PERCEPTION

PERCEPTION

DANIEL J. WEINTRAUB

EDWARD L. WALKER

The University of Michigan

BROOKS/COLE PUBLISHING COMPANY
Belmont, California

A Division of Wadsworth Publishing Company, Inc.

5 6 7 8 9 10—74 73 72 71 70

L. C. cat. card No.: 66-26288

Printed in the United States of America

SERIES FOREWORD

Basic Concepts in Psychology was conceived as a series of brief paperback volumes constituting a beginning textbook in psychology. Several unique advantages arise from publishing individual chapters as separate volumes rather than under a single cover. Each book or chapter can be written by an author identified with the subject matter of the area. New chapters can be added, individual chapters can be revised independently, and, possibly, competitive chapters can be provided for controversial areas. Finally, to a degree, an instructor of the beginning course in psychology can choose a particular set of chapters to meet the needs of his students.

Probably the most important impetus for the series came from the fact that a suitable textbook did not exist for the beginning courses in psychology at the University of Michigan—Psychology 100 (Psychology as a Natural Science) and Psychology 101 (Psychology as a Social Science). In addition, no laboratory manual treated both the natural science and social science problems encountered in the first laboratory course, Psychology 110.

For practical rather than ideological reasons most of the original complement of authors came from the staff of the University of Michigan. As the series has developed, authors have been selected from other institutions in an effort to assure national representation and a broad perspective in contemporary psychology.

Each author in the Basic Concepts in Psychology Series has considerable freedom. He has been charged to devote approximately half of his resources to elementary concepts and half to topics of special interest and emphasis. In this way, each volume will reflect the personality and viewpoint of the author while presenting the subject matter usually found in a chapter of an elementary textbook.

CONTENTS

The term *perception* is usually applied to the way one comes to know the world or the way one experiences the world of objects and events. A standard dictionary describes a *percept* as an impression of an object obtained solely by use of the senses. This definition is satisfactory for most purposes. Real problems arise, however, when one tries to define perception with greater precision. Let us examine these problems briefly: What basis is there for the belief that there is a difference between the real world and the world as we perceive it? What are some of the concrete objectives of studies of the nature of perception? Can reasonable distinctions be made between perception and closely related fields of psychology such as sensory processes, cognition, and neuropsychology? Finally, let us look at the problems associated with the philosophical status of percept and object, and the extent to which the two correspond to each other.

Is the real world as we perceive it to be? Most of us are not naive enough to believe that the world is *exactly* as we perceive it to be. Naive realism represents one extreme of the possible range of correspondence between the real world and our perception of it. As we perceive it, the real world is fundamentally stable and predictable. We see an object, reach for it, and are not surprised when our hand comes into contact with it. If we could not predict events on the basis of our perception of the real world, we would have great difficulty surviving. Our belief in the predictability of real-world events, though justified, sometimes leads us to accept a correspondence between the physical world and perception far beyond that warranted by the facts.

Visual illusion is one realm of experience in which the difference between perception and the physical world becomes quite clear. An example that is rather universally perceived is the moon illusion: the moon appears to be larger when it is near the horizon than when it is directly overhead. One can establish, through physical measurement, that the angle formed at the eye by opposite edges of the moon is the same whether the moon is at the horizon or overhead. The variation in the apparent size of the moon is called an illusion because what seems true when we perceive the moon appears false when we apply physical measurement.

Naive realism is also contradicted by the idea that two people may perceive the *same* situation differently. In other volumes in this series, it is either directly stated or implied that the way a person perceives a situation may be determined by some aspect of his own personality or by social circumstances. In either case, perception implicitly depends on something more than the character of a specific stimulus situation.

There is also the problem of the range of sensory capacities. While such differences in capacity do not call into question the correspondence between the real world and our perception of it, they do lead us to speculate how the world might appear to organisms with capacities different from our own. Some dogs hear sound frequencies far above the upper limits of human hearing. Many appear to have a sense of smell that far exceeds human capacities. On the other hand, dogs seem to be color blind. The dog's perceptual world is probably as stable and predictable as ours, but his perception of the world must be very different. An even more radical difference must exist in certain species of gymnotid fish. These species are nocturnal in their habits and live in water that is frequently very muddy. They have developed the capacity both to send and receive weak electrical signals. Much of their knowledge of the real world comes through a sensing mechanism that is quite outside the universe of man's immediate perceptual experience.

Thus, (1) illusions, demonstrable differences between perception and the facts of physical measurement, (2) apparent differences in perception based on differences in people's characteristics and histories, and (3) what we infer to be very different perceptions of the world by organisms with differing sensory capacities—all make it clear that our perception of the world is something we *construct* from whatever information is available to us.

The *Perceptual Demonstration Kit* that was designed to accompany this text contains many demonstrations and modest experiments that contribute to an appreciation of certain ways perception and the physical properties of a stimulus can fail to correspond. The Kit materials also show the manner in which some stimulus properties, such as the mixture of yellow and blue, can result in unexpected perceptual experiences—in this instance, the experience of gray.

Why study perception? There is a variety of reasons for studying perception. Most fundamentally, man wants to know the nature of the physical world, and he wants to know himself. Many contributions to the field of perception have been and are being made by physical scientists, for they must detect discrepancies between the physical world and our perceptions of it in order to discount errors in observation that arise from perceptual problems. Psychologists can learn about the nature of the perceptual process from such discrepancies.

There are many practical problems that give rise to an analytical interest in perception. Here are some well-known examples: (1) Columns in the Greeks' ancient temples bow outward, so that their diameters are slightly larger half way up than they are at either the top or bottom. Parallel columns, which are perfectly straight cylinders, have the illusory appearance of bowing inward. In order for them to be perceived as straight, it was necessary to construct them with outward curvature. (2) A painter often has the problem of inducing in the perceiver something that is not present in the real world—for example, the perception of depth in a painting that is essentially two dimensional. (3) The technical development of movies and television is largely dependent upon a firm grounding in principles of visual perception.

Principles of perception are becoming increasingly important in efforts to replace human labor by machines. Even though bank officials have surprisingly little difficulty verifying signatures on checks, machine reading of signatures might speed up this process and increase efficiency. To achieve such reading, however, a machine must be designed or programmed to carry out something like the subtle perceptual process of the human observer who now reads and identifies signatures despite wide variations in the signatures written by one person.

The logical status of perception. The terms "awareness" and "consciousness" used in definitions of perception have very subjective implications. One's awareness and one's consciousness are truly one's own. Private experience is unique, and there is no way one can be sure that his private experience is the same as someone else's private experience. Therefore, since most of us think of perception as primarily a matter of private experience, how can perception be studied objectively?

The obvious approach is to obtain and study *descriptions* of perceptual experiences. Perception as a theoretical concept can be developed out of qualitative and quantitative descriptions obtained under a variety of controlled conditions. A theory of perception can then be constructed.

Thus the term *perception* is applied (1) to a wholly subjective experience; (2) to a set of descriptions that are more or less sophisticated in terms of quantification and experimental control; (3) to a theoretical concept; and (4) to a theory of perception. The first, by definition, is not amenable to experimental treatment; the second and third are the subject matter of this volume; the fourth, while sketched in the following chapter, will be left largely to advanced texts.

Much of the literature of perception tends to be theoretical—and for good reasons: (1) Some theories have been developed in an effort to account for limited areas of perceptual phenomena. (2) Other theories have been based on perceptual phenomena and then extended in an effort to integrate all of psychology. (3) Still other theories have been the stimulus for new experiments that have revealed perceptual relationships which had not been explicit before. Examples of various relationships of theory to research are evident in the brief theoretical accounts that follow.

Even though this volume is intended to be a review of *phenomena* of visual perception as revealed in demonstrations and experiments, a brief survey of relevant theories is presented in this chapter to aid the reader in organizing and understanding the material that follows. In the final chapter, an effort will be made to relate some of the phenomena of perception to broader issues in psychology.

GESTALT PSYCHOLOGY

The Gestalt position developed from a consideration of problems of perceptual organization, and it generated both experiments and demonstrations of many perceptual phenomena. The essence of Gestalt psychology is an emphasis on the configurational aspects of perception, on its wholeness. The German word *Gestalt* is often translated to mean *configuration*. The catch phrase of the Gestalt point of view in perception is "the whole is greater than the sum of the parts," and a corollary of this belief is the futility of trying to break down perception into elemental parts. For example, Gestalt theorists pointed out that a musical composition is something more than the musical notes of which it was formed. One could transpose the melody (configuration) to a higher or lower key, keep none of the original notes (elements), and yet preserve the melody. Among the many perceptual phenomena emphasized by Gestalt psychologists are the principles of organization of two-dimensional patterns, discussed in Chapter 3. They also are largely responsible for demonstrating perceptual constancies of size, shape, brightness, and color, to be discussed later.

Gestalt theory embodies a strong element of nativism. It tries to explain the manner in which the world is perceived in terms of the

4

innate structure of the organism. That is, man perceives in a particular fashion because he was born that way. A second characteristic of Gestalt theory is the effort to relate principles of organization of visual perception to a particular conception of cortical functioning. The most important concept, that of "psychoneural isomorphism," asserts that the experience of an object and the representation of that object, in terms of events occurring in the brain, are isomorphic; that is, merely two different ways of looking at the same thing. The cortical processes underlying perception are conceptualized as "force fields," hypothetical forces somewhat akin to the magnetic lines of force surrounding a magnet. Two primary references on Gestalt theory are Köhler (1929) and Prentice (1959).

Gestalt theory placed emphasis on a phenomenological approach to visual perception. This approach led to techniques of arranging visual demonstrations which a person can look at and experience. Many of these are discussed in later chapters, and others have been included in the *Perceptual Demonstration Kit*. Most of the effects of these demonstrations are very easy to experience and very difficult to describe.

SENSORY-TONIC FIELD THEORY

Developed by Werner and Wapner (1952), Sensory-Tonic Field Theory is notable for its strong Gestalt flavor and its concept of equilibrium. The "sensory" in the name of the theory comes from its treatment of the sensory input from an object and from the background, while the "tonic" (as in muscle tonus) refers to input from inside the body— thus, muscles and internal organs. The theory assumes that an interaction exists between stimuli from the external environment and stimuli from within the perceiver. An organism tends to establish a stable state (body equilibrium). If the inputs are not in equilibrium, the result will be a shift in the perceived location of objects, a change in the orientation of the body, or both, until equilibrium is reestablished. Perceptual experience cannot be analyzed into its components because different stimulus inputs can lead to precisely the same perceptual end product.

A set of perceptual experiments to which sensory-tonic theory is especially relevant are those in which the subject's perception of the vertical is the primary variable. In such experiments, a subject might be asked to judge when a rod reaches a vertical position. Judgments have been obtained under a wide variety of conditions, including tilting the subject or even tilting the room in which the subject is seated. The theory assumes that the state of equilibrium can be measured by the difference, if any, between what the subject decides is vertical and the true vertical. Some of these phenomena, which are of special interest both in normal flying and in space flight, are discussed in Chapter 9.

A NEUROPHYSIOLOGICAL THEORY OF PERCEPTION

In the process of creating a general theory of behavior, Hebb (1949) developed a theory of perception that contrasts rather sharply with the Gestalt point of view. Lest the label "neurophysiological" be misleading, it should be pointed out that Hebb's theory places heavy emphasis on psychology. Hebb rejected the nativistic position of the Gestalt psychologists. While they offered an account for the generality of perceptual organization, Hebb felt they could not account for learning. Hebb first tried to isolate the qualities of visual perception that, for example, would be available to a person possessing vision for the first time. Rather than a highly organized configuration attributable to the structure of the organism, Hebb conceived that first visual experience is an impoverished chaos in which objects have nothing more than the quality of *primitive unity*. This concept is an attempt to identify the absolutely minimum distinction a newly seeing organism can make between an object and its surroundings. Primitive unity is, figuratively, the speck of innate capacity initially necessary to allow an organism to distinguish an object. According to Hebb, with repeated visual experience one very slowly learns two additional characteristics of the perception of the object. The first is *nonsensory unity*—meaning the acquired aspects of perception. It is called "nonsensory" because these qualities, Hebb felt, are attributable to learning and are not properties of the stimulus. Primitive unity as the innate aspect and nonsensory unity as the learned aspect of object perception are in sharp contrast with the wholly innate character of perception assumed by Gestalt psychology. According to Hebb, the final characteristic of an object, that of *identity*, represents our capacity to identify an object as one we have seen before, and is learned only after many encounters with the object.

Another way Hebb's theory differs from Gestalt theory is in their accounts of the neurophysiological structure and functioning that underlie behavior, including perceptual phenomena. The Gestalt psychologists had tried to explain perceived stimuli in terms of "fields of force" or "potential difference" across large areas of the brain. In contrast, Hebb undertook to explain the essential characteristics of perception through a plausible account of the development of, and changes in, connections between neurons at the synapses where impulses are passed from one neuron to another. Primitive unity was said to be based on a pattern of firing of individual units in the cortex, which was determined entirely by the pattern of stimulation and the innate structure of the nervous system. With repeated experience of an object, changes would occur in synaptic thresholds, some of the original units would be lost and new ones recruited, and there would be formed a new neural organization called a *cell assembly*. Nonsensory unity could not characterize the perception of an object until a cell assembly had been organized through experience to provide more information than was available in the present stimulus. When objects or events follow each other in time with some consistency, the successive activation of the relevant cell assemblies would tend to knit them together into higher-order patterns of organization called *phase sequences*. The property of *identity* could develop only after the organism had acquired the appropriate phase sequence through experience. Through the development of this set of concepts and others, Hebb felt that he could account for the general properties of the perceptual experience emphasized by the Gestalt psychologists and at the same time account for the stability of learning.

Hebb's theorizing has stimulated a number of programs of research in neurophysiology, and in computer simulation of the nervous system. Of major interest in this volume, however, are the studies of the development of perception, some of which are discussed in later chapters and in another volume in this series (Walker, *Conditioning and Instrumental Learning*).

ADAPTATION-LEVEL THEORY

Adaptation-level theory employs the concept of equilibrium in a manner similar to that of sensory-tonic theory. The perception of a stimulus is assumed to be based on how closely the stimulus properties match the prevailing level of adaptation (equilibrium) of the organism. The adaptation level is influenced by inputs from the immediate environment, including the background, and also by previous inputs. An example is a porch light's appearance, dim by day, bright by night, yet also influenced by whether one has previously been in the illuminated interior of the house or is approaching from the darkened street. The actual intensity of the porch light remains the same throughout, but the intensity which is perceived is presumed to depend upon a change in adaptation level.

Adaptation-level theory has been developed extensively by Helson (1959, 1964). Helson provides mathematical formulas for deriving the equilibrium point in certain cases, and tries to show that what is perceived depends heavily upon whether the object or event in question is above, equal to, or below the adaptation level of the perceiver. The theory intially was developed to account for certain color experiences which occur under unusual illumination conditions (see Chapters 7 and 8 on the perception of color).

Adaptation-level theory, like Gestalt theory, considers the relevance of the total stimulus situation for perceiving. However, adaptation-level theory focuses upon the contribution of individual stimulus elements, and is empiricistic (stresses the influence of past experience), two viewpoints foreign to the Gestalt approach.

PERCEPTUAL PSYCHOPHYSICS

An important theoretical development in perception is the work of Gibson (1950a, 1959). He has been concerned primarily with the perception of depth and distance, which are discussed in Chapter 4. Gibson assumes that a stimulus provides sufficient pieces of information (cues) to the receptors of the eye to account for depth and distance perception. For every perceptual experience, there is an interrelationship (perhaps quite a complex one) among the elements of the stimulus array, to which the perceptual experience can be shown to correspond. Gibson has designed a number of experiments to ferret out these relationships and has contributed to the list of cues that can be shown to aid in depth perception. Gibson's approach emphasizes the need of an observer to *learn* to attend to cues.

PROBABILISTIC FUNCTIONALISM

Brunswik (1955) based the concept of statistical uncertainty in the prediction of behavior upon the assertion of a fundamental discrepancy between perception and behavior. (See also a discussion of Brunswik's theory by Postman and Tolman, 1959.) In the functionalist tradition, the theory stresses the achievement of the organism in adjusting to the environment and the processes involved. A percept is regarded as an inference about the world reached on the basis of cues from the environment. Brunswik felt that even if we could know everything about the stimulus conditions existing in the world and everything about the observer's responses, a perfect prediction about perception could still not be made. One can predict perception from behavior or behavior from perception with only a certain probability of correctness. It is, according to Brunswik, theoretically impossible to have strict laws of perception corresponding to laws of physics.

Brunswik's position with respect to human behavior is a direct contradiction of the deterministic position, which is fundamental to much of the strategic position of experimental psychology. The basic reason for the probabilistic character inherent in perception is that the observer is forced to reconstruct the world "out there" on the basis of information reaching the sense organs. Bodily changes (such as shifts in orientation and position) and changes in the environment (such as the shifting location of objects) prevent the reconstruction from ever being perfectly related to the objects in the environment. Thus the observer is perpetually in the process of making guesses or bets on the basis of uncertain information.

Brunswik's position led him to suggest a different kind of research in perception than any that had been done before. He called it *representative design*. He performed experiments in an observer's day-to-day environment, so that the uncertain and probabilistic cues on which perception is based would be representative of the normal situation. Taking perception into the laboratory, he claimed, destroyed the probabilistic character of information met in the real world. A typical experiment involved accompanying an observer during his usual daily activities and asking for judgments about the size of everyday objects encountered. This procedure captured representative samples of the everyday world in a manner in which a laboratory experiment on size judgments would not. (The problem of size constancy is discussed in Chapter 5.)

PERCEPTUAL READINESS

Whereas "classical" theories of perception tend to address themselves to the character and organization of perception in relative isolation from other concepts and variables of interest to psychologists, a group of newer theories takes motivational and learning variables into account in determining the observer's *readiness* to perceive the world in one manner rather than another. Representative of such theories is that of Bruner (1957). His theory rests on the concept of perceptual categorization. An observer is presumed to categorize stimulus input from his environment by the process of reaching decisions among possible alternative categories. Such a decision is determined not only by the stimulus input but also by what the observer is prepared to perceive. The accessibility of a given category, and thus the likelihood of a given percept, will depend on the observer's past experience, the likelihood of a given input, and the observer's needs. He categorizes (perceives) accordingly. Some of the newer theories and the experiments which are related to motivational and learning variables are discussed in Chapter 10, Perceptual Plasticity.

PERCEPTUAL ORGANIZATION AND THE PERCEPTION OF TWO-DIMENSIONAL PATTERNS

3

Many of the most interesting aspects of normal visual perception can be illuminated through examination of some of the basic problems of the perception of two-dimensional patterns. This chapter is devoted to a consideration of the orientation of the visual image on the retina and to some of the simple principles of perceptual organization. Throughout, the reader should concern himself with the extent to which the nature of the percept is determined by the nature of the real world and by contributions of the observer himself.

ORIENTATION OF THE IMAGE ON THE RETINA

The eye contains a lens system which focuses an image of part of the environment on the light-sensitive retina of the eye. As is true in a camera, the image is inverted in its orientation. (A demonstration of the inverted orientation of the retinal image is contained in the *Perceptual Demonstration Kit*.) A fairly convincing demonstration of the reversed orientation of the retinal image can be carried out without equipment. If you close both eyes and exert a mild pressure on the side of one eye, you will probably see something that looks like a halo. But the halo of light is perceived to be on the opposite side of the visual field from the point of pressure. The pressure is assumed to produce neural excitation near the point of pressure producing the sensation of light. Activity on the right side of the retina is perceived as being on the left side of the visual field.

Since the image must be coded into a pattern of nerve impulses before perception can occur, and since there is no obvious reason why orientation of the image cannot be coded in the process, the orientation of the image on the retina would seem to be of little consequence. Analogously, if one could observe the train of electromagnetic energy proceeding from a television transmitter, it would make little sense. Yet all the necessary information for the television picture is there, ready for decoding by the receiver at home. The decoding process can be arranged to present the picture in any orientation. Similarly, perception can be thought of as processes of encoding and decoding. The code of impulses in the visual system contains a great deal of the information reaching the retina. Each time the head, eyes, or objects in the environment move, the coded information changes accordingly. The vertical and horizontal orientation of the image is only one small aspect of the organizing of information carried out by the perceiver.

FIGURE AND GROUND

Probably the most basic organization imposed on the world by the observer is that which leads to the perception of objects as seeming to stand out against a background. The technical term for this phenomenon is the *figure-ground* relationship. Demonstration 32 in the demonstration kit illustrates two of the traditional figure-ground reversible figures. One of these is reproduced in Figure 3.1. Either a vase or faces can be seen,

Figure 3.1

A reversible figure.

but not both at the same time. If the vase is perceived, it becomes the figure, and the remainder of the picture becomes ground. If the faces are seen as figure, the body of the vase becomes a part of the ground.

Distinctions between figure and ground were stated explicitly by Edgar Rubin (1921; English translation, 1958), who listed seven differences between figure and ground: (1) When two fields have a common border, it is the figure which seems to have shape while the ground does not. (2) The ground seems to extend behind the figure. (3) The figure appears to be object-like (even though it may be an abstract shape) while the ground does not. (4) The color of the figure seems more substantial and solid than that of the ground. (5) The ground tends to be perceived as farther away and the figure nearer the observer even though both are obviously at the same distance. (6) The figure is more dominant and impressive and tends to be remembered more easily. (7) The common border between figure and ground is called a contour, and the contour appears to be a property of figures.

The Gestalt position would be that Rubin's seven distinctions are characteristic of perception because of the inherent structure of all organisms. According to Hebb, such distinctions would be learned slowly through repeated experience. In essence, Hebb's property of primitive unity refers to the very germ of the experience of figures as separable from their backgrounds. When we have had sufficient visual experience so that the seven properties develop through the establishment of cell assemblies, then the figure can be said to attain nonsensory unity. Primitive unity is unlearned, while nonsensory unit is learned. The perceptual characteristic of identity represents, for Hebb, an even higher form of perceptual learning.

THE "LAW OF PRÄGNANZ"

The "Law of Prägnanz" is another basic law of perceptual organization as promulgated by the Gestalt psychologists. The usual translation is "good configuration" or simply "good figure." The idea is that the perceiver will organize his perception of the environment so that the environment appears as simple and as orderly as possible. Like most Gestalt principles, this one is assumed to be an innate characteristic of the organism, and to be simultaneously a characteristic of the perception and the brain process associated with the perceptual experience. The "law" itself is rather vague and difficult to specify. "Good" figures are assumed to have the properties of simplicity, symmetry, balance, and ease of being remembered. A geometric square seems to satisfy these properties; an irregular figure does not.

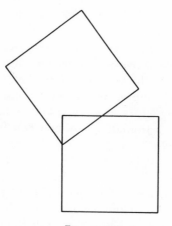

Figure 3.2

The influence of good configuration.

Do you perceive the figure in Figure 3.2 as two overlapping squares? There are other ways they could be perceived—for example, as three irregular figures. Squares, however, are in some sense better figures than irregular figures. Therefore, the tendency is to see squares.

There are a number of other principles of perceptual organization, each of which applies primarily to the perception of two-dimensional figures and many of which might be regarded as corollaries of the Law of Prägnanz.

Closure. The principle of closure states that there is a tendency to perceive an incomplete figure as the complete figure of which it appears to be a part. Figure 3.3 contains two incomplete figures. One appears

Figure 3.3

Examples of closure.

to be a circle, and the other appears to be a horse and rider. Both, though obviously incomplete, can be identified. Closure can be demonstrated by a simple procedure. If the incomplete circle, for example, is flashed briefly on a screen, a subject, when asked to draw what he saw, will often reproduce a complete circle. The tendency to perceive it as a complete circle, and thus close the gap, accounts for the name of the principle.

Familiarity. Experiments have shown that if relatively unfamiliar figures are presented to observers who are asked at some later date to reproduce them, the reproduction tends to look somewhat more like familiar figures than did the original figures shown. Familiarity depends upon past learning and has therefore not been emphasized by Gestalt psychologists because of their emphasis on nativism. Nonetheless, familiarity is an important principle.

LAWS OF GROUPING

A set of elements tends to become organized in perception. The elements tend not to be seen as isolated but to be grouped. Wertheimer (English translation, 1958) has presented principles termed the laws of grouping. They include the following:

Proximity. Elements which are in the proximity of other elements or which are near each other tend to be seen as belonging to each other. We tend to see the x's of Figure 3.4 as eight pairs of x's rather than as sixteen x's.

x x   x x   x x   x x   x x   x x   x x   x x

Figure 3.4

An illustration of proximity.

Similarity. When other factors are equal, elements similar to each other are grouped together to the exclusion of dissimilar elements. The x's and o's in Figure 3.5 tend to form columns rather than rows.

o   x   o   x   o   x

o   x   o   x   o   x

o   x   o   x   o   x

o   x   o   x   o   x

o   x   o   x   o   x

Figure 3.5

An illustration of similarity.

Good continuation. Items tend to be grouped together because they seem to continue the characteristic direction of previous elements. In Figure 3.6, one tends to see two smooth curves of dots from *A* to *C* and from *B* to *D*. This way of seeing the figure would illustrate good continuation.

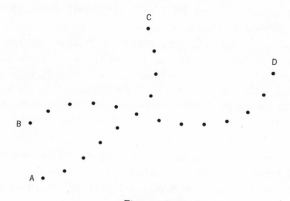

Figure 3.6

An illustration of good continuation.

Common fate. Good continuation refers to the grouping of elements. Common fate refers to elements actually in motion. Elements moving in

a common direction relative to other elements tend to be grouped together. Suppose that alternate x's in Figure 3.7 were moving downward

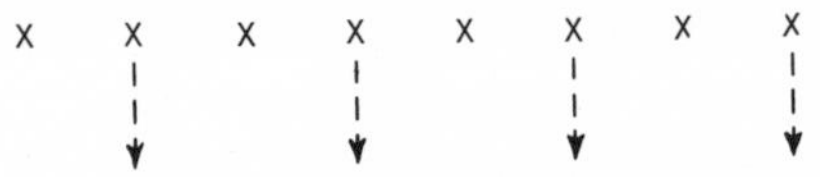

X   X   X   X   X   X   X   X

Figure 3.7

The principle of common fate.

together, in the direction of the arrows and at the same rate. Those in
motion would tend to be perceived as a group and would illustrate the
principle of common fate.

Apparent motion. The "motion" in "motion pictures" is only "apparent motion," since a movie is a sequence of still pictures. Apparent
motion can also be produced by proper arrangement and timing of
illumination of spots of light. Two lights, for example, can be arranged
to blink alternately (with proper spatial separation, timing sequence,
light intensity, etc.), so that the observer perceives one light moving
back and forth across the intervening distance. This apparent motion is
called the *phi phenomenon*. It is only one of several forms of motion
perceived in situations in which no actual motion occurs. The laboratory
study of apparent motion was begun in 1910 by Wertheimer, who was
one of the originators of Gestalt psychology.

Considerable theoretical concern and disagreement have developed
concerning the nature of the cortical processes involved in apparent motion. For a review of the problem, as well as a review of forms of apparent
motion other than the phi phenomenon, the reader can consult Osgood
(1953, pps. 243–248).

PRINCIPLES OF ORGANIZATION IN OPPOSITION

Principles of organization may be pitted against one another experimentally to determine their relative strengths.

In Figure 3.8, *good continuation* and *good figure* are working in
opposition. It may therefore be seen as either two squares or a single

Figure 3.8

The grouping of elements as good figures.

figure. In Figure 3.9, closure may operate even though proximity is unfavorable for such grouping. In Figure 3.10, proximity and similarity have been placed in some degree of opposition. Do you see rows or

Figure 3.9

Closure can lead to two groups of elements.

X O X O X O X O X O X O X

X O X O X O X O X O X O X

X O X O X O X O X O X O X

X O X O X O X O X O X O X

X O X O X O X O X O X O X

Figure 3.10

Proximity versus similarity.

columns, or do they oscillate? The relative influence of the two factors can be measured when the horizontal elements are moved different distances apart. Which principles are contrasted in Figure 3.11? When

Figure 3.11

Proximity versus closure.

more than one principle is operating, and their effects would lead to different groupings, a balanced arrangement leads sometimes to different groupings and sometimes to alternation between groupings. The effect is similar to the reversible figures such as the vase-faces in Figures 3.1 (or the Schröder Staircase in Experiment 33 of the demonstration kit).

The principles of perceptual organization that have been reviewed are intuitively compelling and appear to have a degree of usefulness—a usefulness, however, confined largely to their application to problems of two-dimensional displays such as advertising, painting, and motion pictures. Except in a very few instances, scientifically oriented investigations have not developed, and the information available on principles of two-dimensional visual perception, such as those outlined in the preceding pages, has remained relatively static.

PERCEPTUAL ORGANIZATION: ACQUIRED OR INNATE?

Unlike the principles of perceptual organization, which have excited little further experimental interest, the nativism of the Gestalt psychologists probably contributed to an already present and avid interest in the problem. An experimental approach is made somewhat difficult by the very importance of human visual perception. There is an understandable reluctance on the part of experimenters to interfere in any way with the development of perception in the human infant, and a degree of daring is inherent in experiments which undertake to distort human visual perception in order to observe the nature of the adjustment process. Animals have limited usefulness because they cannot communicate very much about their private perceptual experience. In spite of all these difficulties, useful information has been collected.

Human babies are occasionally born with congenital cataracts. When the defect is severe, it is probable that visual experience is limited to changes in general illumination and has very little pattern quality. When such cataracts are removed through surgery, after the child is old enough to be fully articulate, one would seem to have an ideal opportunity to collect data on the nature of perceptual organization which is without benefit of much prior experience. Unfortunately, such data are usually obtained casually and are not easy to interpret. Adequate tests are difficult to devise, and it is rarely possible to determine the precise nature of the visual experiences prior to surgery.

A collection of such cases dating back to the middle of the eighteenth century has been collected and published by Von Senden (1932) and recently reviewed and analyzed by Hebb (1949). It is reported that these patients could not identify patterns, objects, or faces when first exposed to them. They were able to identify objects by touch, but touching and feeling the object while looking at it on one occasion was not sufficient to produce identification through vision on a subsequent presentation. A rather long period of learning was necessary to produce visual recognition. Some individuals maintained poor visual recognition of complex shapes, such as human faces, even after many months of visual experience. It is also reported that visual acuity, the capacity to discriminate small visual details, was essentially normal.

A degree of verification of the results of studies of the human "congenital cataract" cases comes from the work of Riesen (1958) with chimpanzees. Chimpanzees were raised in the dark from birth until they were well developed physically. When these animals were then exposed to light, they behaved pretty much as a blind person would, and they were later shown to have retinas which did not develop properly. In order to prevent degeneration of the visual system, other chimpanzees were raised in the dark but given daily exposures to unpatterned light with their heads enclosed in frosted plastic domes. When these animals were permitted full vision, they were initially unable to fixate on objects normally, and they were very slow in learning problems that required them to discriminate between objects or other visual patterns. In other words, the chimpanzees behaved very much as one might expect if the nature of their defect was similar to that reported in the human cataract cases.

Optical prisms can be devised for human subjects. Such prisms, when worn, invert the image reaching the eye, so that the floors appear to be up and the ceilings down. This experiment was first done by Stratton (1897). He reported that there was a slow learning of the inverted orientation over a period of weeks. When the prisms were removed, restoration of normal orientation also required considerable time. Kohler (1962) in more recent experiments used prisms which added color fringes at borders and made straight lines appear curved. The curvatures were such that the appearance of lines changed with every movement of the eyes and head. Subjects reported that the world looked as if it were made of rubber. After several weeks, subjects adapted to the color and curvature effects, and again perceived a stable world. When the prisms were removed, aftereffects were experiencd that lasted for several days. Phantom color fringes appeared, and straight lines appeared curved in the direction opposite to the curvature that had been produced by the prisms. Somehow, the visual system learns to adjust to a constantly changing distortion of input, and this distortion persists after the prisms are removed, leading to reverse distortions. Such experiments do not establish that perceptual orientations are learned originally, but they do make it clear that these orientations can be radically influenced by learning.

As might be expected, not all of the evidence in recent experimental work favors the point of view that the organized and dynamic qualities of perception are acquired or learned. Hubel and Wiesel (1963) and Wiesel and Hubel (1963), using kittens as experimental animals, have made electrical recordings from single nerve cells in the visual cortex while very simple patterns were being presented to the eyes. Some nerve cells will produce a response only when a line with a characteristic tilt is in the visual field. The experimenters report that the cell will continue to respond even when the line is moved across the visual field as long as the orientation of the line does not change. Such cells are thus very likely involved in complex pattern perception as contrasted with punctiform stimulation.

Hubel and Wiesel also report that such cells will respond very early after birth, but response abnormalities develop if the kitten is deprived of patterned light. Very young kittens were found to be quite susceptible to the effects of early visual deprivation. In accord with Riesen's observations with chimpanzees, after early deprivation a kitten would bump into chairs, step into platters of milk, fall off tables, and generally behave as if it were blind. The implication is that the neural mechanisms necessary for pattern vision develop independently of stimulation and thus are not learned. But they then become defective if patterned vision is not permitted.

Thus the roles played by maturation and experience in the development of patterned vision are not simple and not likely to be easily resolved. The problem of perceptual learning in a context other than the nature-nurture controversy in perceptual development will be discussed again in Chapter 10, Perceptual Plasticity.

DEPTH PERCEPTION

That we experience the world as three dimensional is beyond question. Not only does the world "appear" to us to be a three-dimensional space filled with objects at different distances, but we can perform acts requiring exceedingly accurate judgments of depth, such as catching a ball. Contemplate the skill of the airline captain landing a jet liner. His judgment of distance must be accurate in terms of height and distance from the runway, and as he brings the aircraft in for a landing, accuracy within a few inches is required. Observations of the play of champion sportsmen frequently reveal need for depth judgments to small fractions of an inch. Such skilled individuals demonstrate that the capacity to perceive depth is truly extensive and precise.

The eye is impressive in its capacities but appears to be badly engineered for any of its tasks. The retina hugs the curved rear surface of the eye. The focused image falls on areas of this surface, which varies in sensitivity and is fairly flat except for a depression, the fovea, in its center. There is nothing about the structure of the retina that suggests a means to achieve three-dimensional perception. In fact, the eye would seem to be ill-suited for seeing in even two dimensions. The image has been brought into focus by a lens system which does not meet modern optical standards. Blurring of the image occurs because the lens system bends different wavelengths of light differently (chromatic aberration), and because of an incorrect over-all curvature of the lens (spherical aberration). These aberrations are common to all human eyes. Cellular debris in the more or less transparent fluids of the eye further degrades the image, and surprisingly, the retina seems to have been put in backwards. Before the light can reach and excite the receptors, which are pointing away from the incoming light, it must pass first through blood vessels and nerve fibers lying on the front surface of the retina. Good design would seem to dictate that these retinal structures should lie behind, not in front of, the receptors. The eye is constantly in motion, changing fixation from location to location, making very small movements, including slow drifting, rapid jerks, and a jittering back and forth at rates up to 150 times per second. The tiny retinal receptors record a mosaic of the original scene much like the fine dot structure of facsimile newspaper photographs. The retinal mosaic even has a gap in it, called the optic dics, at the point where the nerve fibers come together to form the optic nerve. Receptors are absent in this area—approximately 5 millimeters toward the nose and slightly up from center of the retina. If only one eye is open, no representation of the environment is present from an area subtending about 7 degrees of the visual field (the so-called blind spot); yet that area is somehow perceived as filled in (see Experiment 15 in the demonstration kit). The visual system does a remarkable job, even though its structural properties appear less than ideally suited.

It seems likely that having two eyes which usually focus on the same object should contribute greatly to the perception of three-dimensions, although the way this happens is a mystery. Even though some depth can be seen monocularly, a question remains. How can the organism take one flat image from one eye, combine it with another flat image from the other eye, and produce a perception with an added quality of depth that neither image possesses?

Efforts to solve the problem can be divided into three categories: (1) efforts to think it through without gathering additional information, (2) efforts to find ways to simulate or illustrate three dimensions, and (3) efforts to demonstrate the role of presumed factors by experiments. The first is the approach of the philosopher; the second, primarily that of the artist; the third, that of the experimental psychologist.

THE PHILOSOPHICAL APPROACH

Of the many aspects of the problem of the perception of three dimensions that could be subject to philosophical analysis, two closely intertwined questions stand out. The first is related to the sensory basis of three-dimensional perception, and the second is the question of the extent to which perception of depth is inherent in the structure of the organism and thus innately given, and the extent to which the perception of depth is acquired through experience.

As the question has been posed to you, the visual system does not appear capable of yielding three-dimensional images. A similar assessment led Bishop Berkeley (1709) to look for a solution in other sense qualities. He reasoned that the only sensory modality that appears to yield information that is inherently three dimensional is the sense of touch and motion (kinesthesia). Therefore, the perception of visual depth must be derived from sensations arising from these sources. Furthermore, Berkeley pointed out that the muscles in and around the eye are a source of information. *Accommodation,* the change in curvature of the lens of the eye to focus an image of the object on the retina, can occur when one looks at a very close object, and one can become aware of muscular straining, with efforts to accommodate to a close distance. Also, the external eye muscles bring the eyes inward as an object approaches, a process known as *convergence.* While these sources of sensory information are not inherently three dimensional, Berkeley felt that perhaps, through association with sensory information from the hands and movements of the arms, they came to be interpreted in terms of distance at close range.

Berkeley felt that other cues of distance, such as those used by painters, are based on experience, and thus are learned. In addition to accommodation and convergence as cues of distance, Berkeley added one visual cue to the list. When an object is brought too close to the eye, it becomes blurred in appearance because the accommodation mechanism has failed. Thus Berkeley contributed three cues, two of them nonvisual, and took the position that our perception of distance is learned from these.

Sharply contrasting points of view concerning the extent to which characteristics of perception are acquired or are innate were argued at length by philosophers who were contemporary with or followed Berkeley. Thus Leibnitz (1714) provided a philosophical background for the nativism of Gestalt psychology in Germany, and Diderot (1749) and Condillac (1754) developed a strong philosophical position favoring the construction of perception out of one's own experience. This French tradition of empiricism serves as an intellectual context for Hebb's position on the issue as it was discussed in Chapter 2.

While philosophical argument and analysis are revealing, they by no means exhaust the approaches to the problems. Even if one takes the point of view that the perception of depth is an innately given characteristic of human existence, as does Leibnitz, the search for the structure upon which depth perception is based still remains. If one takes the position, as does Condillac, that we learn to see depth, one is faced with a series of questions to be answered. If we learn to see depth, what is the source of the original perception of depth? How is the learning accomplished? In terms of stimulus characteristics, what are the cues that we use? What are the characeristics of the visual environment which trigger the experience of depth?

THE ARTIST'S APPROACH

The arrangement of materials on a two-dimensional surface in a pattern that produces a three-dimensional effect is the task of the graphic artist. By analogy, his task is similar to that of the psychologist trying to discover how the perception of depth can arise from stimulus patterns falling on a two-dimensional retina. Artists have attacked the problem for centuries and have accumulated a large body of knowledge and technical skill.

The history of the development of depth in paintings is a fascinating problem about which much is known, but about which there is much yet to be determined. The gross pattern of development is discernible in the reproductions contained in this book. The two wall paintings are representative of a great many similar paintings from Egypt, the island of Crete, and other archeological sites. They present an essentially flat appearance and are virtually devoid of depth. The reproductions of the work of Giotto, Masaccio, Raphael, and Canaletto, as well as the modern photograph of the Buddha of Kamakura, yield varying degrees of depth. Braque's *The Pink Tablecloth* again returns to the flatness of the ancient wall paintings. Essentially, those paintings probably result from a lack of knowledge of how to create the experience of depth on a two-dimensional surface; the later paintings, beginning in the thirteenth century, illustrate the development of knowledge; and the Braque illustrates the use of that knowledge to eliminate the appearance of depth. Analysis of these paintings requires an understanding of the cues which contribute to the perception of depth.

THE CUES OF DEPTH THAT CAN BE PORTRAYED ON A TWO-DIMENSIONAL SURFACE

The perception of *size* and the perception of depth are so closely related that some effort is required to distinguish between them. Figure 4.1 contains three triangles that differ only in size. If the reader will contemplate this set of triangles, he is likely to find that at some moments the largest triangle appears to be closest, and the smallest farthest away.

Figure 4.1

Size as a cue of depth.

At other moments, they may all appear to lie on the same plane. When they appear on the plane, they will appear to differ in size. When they appear at different distances, they may appear to be identical in size or at least more nearly the same size than is actually the case.

This shifting effect illustrates a basic point. If objects such as these are perceived to be the same size, they will be seen at different distances. If they are perceived as differing in size, the distance effect will be lost.

A cue of depth, so obvious that it is rarely mentioned, is the cue that arises from the *partial overlap* or interposition of objects when a near object partially obscures the view of a more distant object. This effect can be seen in Figure 4.2. The power of this cue can be seen in Demonstration II contained in the *Perceptual Demonstration Kit*. Two

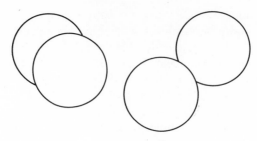

Figure 4.2

Partial overlap as a cue of depth.

playing cards are arranged so that the far card appears to overlap the nearer one. In this situation, partial overlap as a cue of depth takes precedence, and the two cards are perceived as differing in size.

It is apparent that the Cretan painter who produced the *Sacred Grove and Dance* in Plate I did not manipulate the size of objects to create a distance effect, and may not have been aware of the technique. In the Egyptian wall painting *Hunting in a Papyrus Thicket*, the size of figures has been used to portray the relative social importance of the people. For example, the largest female figure is obviously the most important female present. The smallest female figures appear to be servants. Two female figures are drawn to be equal in size, even though one is on the boat and the second is some distance away on the bank of the stream. Thus, early painters appear not to have known how to use size as a depth cue and occasionally used relative size to indicate other characteristics, such as social importance. It will also be noted that partial overlap is avoided wherever possible, apparently to avoid obscuring any part of a figure.

Exactly when the techniques for portraying depth were developed, and by whom they were developed, is not altogether clear. That they appeared in a relatively short interval during the rennaissance in Italian art between the thirteenth and fifteenth centuries is certain. Giovanni Cimabue (1240–1302) is sometimes cited as the father of Italian painting, and the flatness of earlier Italian painting began to disappear in his work. Others choose Giotto di Bondone (1267?–1337). Certainly Giotto's *Angel Appearing to St. Anna* (1305) produces a perception of depth. (See Plate II.) The ambiguity concerning the origin of techniques of portraying depth arises from incomplete examination of earlier Greek, Byzantine, and Eastern art. There is a mosaic from the wall of Cicero's house that was placed there during the first century by a traveling Greek artist called Dioskourides of Samos. That mosaic, *The Street Musicians*, contains depth effects produced with considerable skill.

*Giotto. Life of the Virgin and Christ.
Angel Appearing to St. Anna. (1305)*

*Canaletto. View of St. Mark's Square
In Venice. (1697 - 1768)*

Hunting in a Papyrus Thicket. Tomb of Menna, Thebes. Egyptian. 18th Dynasty (1567 - 1320 B.C.)

Sacred Grove and Dance. Cretan Greek. (1700 - 1580 B.C.)

*Masaccio. Virgin and Child with St.
Anna. (1401 - 1428)*

*Raphael. Transfiguration (detail).
(1483 - 1520)*

Braque. The Pink Tablecloth. (1933)

The Great Buddha at Kamakura.

Whatever their origin, most of the techniques were well developed and well known by the time of Leonardo da Vinci (1452–1519). Leonardo was both articulate and experimental. He distinguished between attached and cast shadow as cues of depth. *Attached shadow* refers to the shadows cast by the contours of an object upon the object itself. The primary cue for revealing the relief of an object are the subtle details of attached shadow. Such shadows can be seen in profusion in the paintings such as that of Raphael in Plate III, while they are absent from the wall paintings of Plate I. *Cast shadow* was distinguished by Leonardo as a separate cue. These two cues can be seen independently in pure form in Figures 4.3 and 4.4.

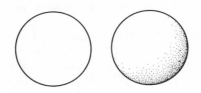

Figure 4.3

Attached shadow as a cue of depth.

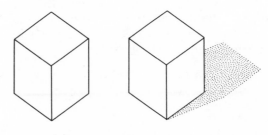

Figure 4.4

Cast shadow as a cue of depth.

Leonardo shows both his articulateness and his experimental approach, writing of aerial perspective as cues of depth (1500; as cited in Woodworth, 1938):

> The air tints distant objects in proportion to their distance from the eye. . . . If you wish to try out this perspective of variation and loss of color, go into the country, select objects situated at distances of 100, 200 yards, etc.,—objects such as trees, houses, men—and as respects the nearest tree, place a sheet of glass firmly in front of you, keep the eye fixed in location, and trace the outlines of the tree on the glass. Now move the glass to the side just enough to allow the tree to be seen beside its tracing, and color your drawing to duplicate the color and relief of the object,

so that when examined with one eye the drawing and the tree shall both seem painted at the same distance. Follow the same procedure in painting the second and third trees situated at the greater distances. Preserve these paintings on glass as aids and teachers in your work.

Suppose several buildings are visible over a wall which conceals their basis, and suppose they all extend to the same apparent height above the wall. You wish to make one appear in your painting more distant than another. Conceive the air to be rather hazy, since in such air you know that distant objects like the mountains, seen through a great mass of air, appear almost blue. . . . Therefore paint the first building beyond the aforesaid wall in its own proper color and make the more distant building less sharply outlined and bluer, and a building that is twice as far away, make it twice as blue, and one that you wish to appear five times as far away, make it five times as blue. This rule will make it possible to tell from the picture which building is farther away and which is taller.

At least three specific depth cues are clear in these passages from Leonardo. The instruction to paint "the more distant building less sharply outlined" can be taken as an operational definition of *detail perspective*. Near objects can be seen in fine detail. As distance increases, the angle subtended by small elements falls below the limits of visual acuity, and the amount of detail the observer can discern decreases. Far objects retain only their gross structure. This cue, detail perspective, has been dealt with extensively by James J. Gibson (1950a), who considers the *texture gradient* a fundamental characteristic of spatial perception. Figure 4.5, taken from Gibson, illustrates the appearance of detail perspective or the texture gradient in relatively pure form.

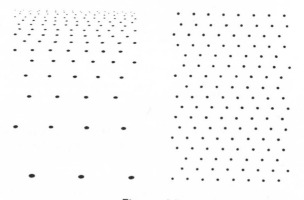

Figure 4.5

Illustration of the texture gradients as a cue of depth. The diagram is a construction based on the geometry of the texture gradient. The two spot distributions yield impressions of a longitudinal and a frontal surface. (Reprinted from Gibson, J. J., The Perception of the Visual World, 1950, by permission of Houghton Mifflin Company.)

Aerial perspective can be seen as having two elements that are closely intertwined: change in the saturation of colors and change in hue. Haze, and all air is hazy to some degree, scatters light. As it is scattered, colors become desaturated, less pure than they would otherwise appear. (Saturation is defined more precisely in Chapter 7.) In a painting, this effect would be simulated by the addition of an appropriate amount of gray paint. The more gray, the more desaturation of the colors, and the greater the apparent distance of the object. This cue of depth might be called *aerial perspective through desaturation.*

Leonardo added blue in proportional amounts to create the effect of distance. In most instances, the specification of blue is appropriate, but the more general rule would be the instruction to add proportional amounts of the hue of the ambient illumination. There are times of the day in some areas of the world during which the sky becomes predominantly red rather than blue. When the sky becomes red, more distant objects would require the addition of red rather than blue to achieve their actual appearance.

The detail from Raphael's *Transfiguration,* in Plate III, contains all three cues to some degree. The decrease in the amount of detail painted into the sequence of faces is quite apparent. That the colors used in the more remote faces are both desaturated and contain more blue is also clear. Showing the face of the epileptic boy in an unnatural light serves to enhance the depth effect among the figures. Most readers will have seen many colored landscape photographs in which these three cues—detail perspective, aerial perspective through desaturation, and aerial perspective through the addition of the hue of the ambient illumination, usually blue—are clearly illustrated.

Linear perspective refers to the fact that parallel lines converge as a function of distance in a two-dimensional geometrical representation of three-dimensional space. In drawing, linear perspective is frequently handled by choosing a "vanishing point" upon which receding lines which are in reality parallel will converge. The linear perspective in Giotto's *Angel Appearing to St. Anna* in Plate II is intuitive; it has an awry appearance. Credit for the development of the geometry of linear perspective, or at least credit for being one of the first to apply it, is usually given to the Italian architect Filippo Brunelleschi (1379–1446). Thereafter, it is certain that painters were able to handle linear perspective with great precision and even distort it to create desired effects. The *View of St. Mark's Square in Venice* by Antonio Canaletto (1697–1768) is famous for several reasons, among which is the fact that it is possible to view this square today from the point at which the artist must have stood. It is reproduced here (see Plate II) because it is a striking example of the precise use of linear perspective. The interested student may wish to try a little further exploration of the structure of this painting. Fasten a small piece of tissue paper over Plate II. Draw at least two lines on each side of the painting to correspond to building lines that are obviously parallel in reality. You will find that the lines you have drawn do not converge on a single point. Instead, the two sets of lines cross each other before the members of each set intersect. With a little imagination, one can visualize what the painting would have looked like had Canaletto used a single vanishing point. The far end of the square would have appeared much farther away, and the far ends of the two sides would have been painted much smaller and in less detail. Canaletto, with full knowledge of the mathematics of linear perspective, made use of that knowledge to make his picture more interesting, and possibly more natural in appearance, than would have been the case had he made faithful use of a single vanishing point.

It is to be noted that while linear perspective and detail perspective are closely related, they are not identical. Neither of the examples in Figure 4.5 shows obvious linear perspective, and in Gibson's experiment, to be discussed later in this chapter, detail perspective or the texture gradient was manipulated while linear perspective as a cue of depth was excluded.

A cue that has a very small effect on the perception of distance is the difference in the apparent distance of "warm" as opposed to "cold" colors. The demonstration kit provides material that can be used to produce the effect by placing appropriately chosen color chips side by side on a homogeneous surface. If one is a warm red or orange and the other is a colder blue or green, one can usually perceive the warmer color as appearing to lie in a plane somewhat nearer the observer than the apparent plane of the colder color. While the effect of this *color cue* of depth is small, it is occasionally used in painting with dramatic effect. An excellent example may be seen in the painting *Virgin and Child with St. Anna* by Masaccio (Tommado Guidi, 1402–1429), which is reproduced in Plate III. The colder blue tones of the Virgin's garment tend to make the figure recede perceptually, while the warmer red tones of the garments of St. Anna tend to make them move forward perceptually. The net effect is to enhance the perception of St. Anna surrounding and mothering the Virgin. If you can imagine exchanging the colors of the two garments, you may see that the essential character of the painting would be lost almost entirely. (The effect may possibly depend upon chromatic aberration in the eye lens. See Evans [1948, p. 323] for an explanation.)

Another visual cue of depth that, while real, is difficult to demonstrate is the effect of *filled versus unfilled space*. Careful and repeated viewing of Figure 4.6 may yield the perception that the filled circle appears either larger, closer, or both, than the circle containing the figure. While this cue is relatively unimportant in painting, it can be isolated and studied experimentally.

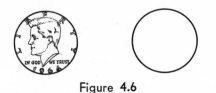

Figure 4.6

*The two circles are actually identical in size, yet the
filled circle may appear both larger and closer as a
function of the fact that the space is filled.*

A final cue that could be used in paintings, though it rarely is, is the
blurring of objects too close to the observer to be in focus. This is a cue
described by Bishop Berkeley. If one stands a foot or two from a window
and looks out, focusing on a distant object, those portions of the window
frame that are at the periphery of vision will be out of focus and blurry.
Hold a pencil near one eye, fixate on a distant object, and the pencil
will appear blurred. This effect is occasionally seen in photographs when
the picture is deliberately framed by near objects while the focus is on
a more distant scene. The photograph of the *Buddha of Kamakura*,
shown in Plate IV, is an illustration. The evergreen trees in the foreground are deliberately out of focus to provide a meaningful and con-
tributory frame for the main objects of interest, the Buddha and the
people in the foreground.

BINOCULAR CUES OF DEPTH

The essential role of binocular vision in the perception of depth
was worked out by Leonardo da Vinci (c. 1500). In working out the
cues of depth that could be used in paintings, he went on to determine
the nature of those cues available in normal vision which could not be
represented on a two-dimensional surface.

The constellation of factors associated with the perception of three
dimensions in binocular vision is usually referred to as *binocular parallax*.
Leonardo pointed out that it is possible to see behind near objects. Figure
4.7 is a reproduction of a drawing of Leonardo's about which he said
(Woodworth, 1938, p. 652ff.):

It is impossible that a painting, though reproducing its object with
absolute perfection of line, light, shade and color, can appear with the
same relief as the natural object—unless indeed that natural object be
seen at a distance and with only one eye. The proof is as follows: Let the
eyes *a* and *b* regard the object *e*, with convergence of the central lines
of sight, *ae* and *be* meeting at point *e;* the lateral lines of vision will pass
beside the object and see space behind it. Eye *a* sees the whole space
fd, eye *b* the whole space *gc*. Together the eyes see the whole space *fc*
behind the object. For this cause the object is transparent, according to

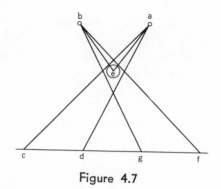

Figure 4.7

Demonstration of the manner in which one may see all of the space behind a near object, as drawn by Leonardo da Vinci.

the definition of a transparent object—behind which nothing is hidden—but this cannot happen to one who looks with only one eye (unless the object is smaller than the pupil of the eye). Thus we have an answer to our question. For in painting, a near object preempts the whole space behind it, and there is no way of making any part of this space visible.

Leonardo's drawing could also be used to demonstrate *binocular disparity,* which refers to the fact that the views of the object obtained by two eyes are not identical. This can be proved geometrically, and it can be demonstrated to one's self easily by examining a small, closely held object first with one eye and then with the other. Two illusions in the perception kit, the floating-finger illusion and the hole-in-palm illusion (Demonstrations 17 and 18), take advantage of the difference in the images provided by each eye. The physicist Charles Wheatstone pointed out this difference in work published in 1838.

Wheatstone developed several devices which permitted independent control of the images seen by the two eyes. He called the first a stereoscope. The depth effect produced by this device had a vivid character not seen in two-dimensional painting, no matter how well constructed; and Wheatstone concluded that binocular disparity was the primary cue of depth. The evidence he presented was as follows:

1. A strong depth effect occurs when two disparate images are obtained through use of the stereoscope.

2. No depth effect occurs when the two views are identical.

3. The depth effect is reversed when the two images are reversed.

4. When the images are made somewhat more disparate than would normally be obtained by the two eyes, the depth effect is exaggerated.

The stereoscope became a fixture in the nineteenth-century parlor, and most libraries stocked large numbers of stereoscopic photos. The modern stereoscopic camera and the stereoscopic viewer are a direct development. Modern binoculars increase the depth effect by separating the primary lenses by a distance greater than the separation of the normal eyes. Several fairly common trick depth effects are occasionally seen, all of which depend upon the disparate images of binocular parallax. If two disparate images are printed on a single sheet, one in red and one in green, and they are slightly misaligned with respect to the horizontal rather than superimposed, a person viewing the picture with a red filter on one eye and a green on the other will perceive depth. One eye receives one of the printed images; the other eye receives the other image. Such a principle was once used to make 3-D movies—the moviegoer was issued a pair of goggles with one green lens and one red when he entered the theater. The same effects have been achieved by means of polarized light, with each of the disparate images photographed and projected with light polarized in different planes, and the viewer equipped with appropriate polarizing filters. A trick that has been used by some magazines requires sophisticated technological achievements— it involves disparate scenes, each chopped into extremely thin vertical strips. The strips, arranged so that every other strip belongs to the same scene, are bonded under clear plastic containing minute vertical ridges. The view meant for the left eye can be seen only through the left side of every ridge; the view for the right eye can be seen only through the right side of the ridges. The effect is depth based on binocular disparity. If such pictures are rotated 90 degrees, the disparity and the depth effect disappear.

Binocular parallax yields still another possible cue of depth because the images of objects closer than the point of fixation are seen as *crossed*, while those beyond the point of fixation are seen as *uncrossed*. The diagram in Figure 4.8 illustrates the geometry of the situation that produces such images. Ordinarily, crossed and uncrossed images are ignored or suppressed, so that we are not aware of them. That we can become aware of them is easily demonstrated. It is only necessary to line up a pencil tip between the eyes and an object about a foot away and shift fixation back and forth between the pencil tip and the object to observe the situation portrayed in Figure 4.8.

Two other forms of parallax yield strong cues of depth, although neither requires the use of two eyes. The first of these is called *head-movement parallax*. If you will close one eye and move the head from side to side through the same distance as the pupils of the two eyes are apart, all of the geometry of binocular parallax will be reproduced in successive rather than simultaneous images. In fact, head-movement parallax can produce an exaggeration of binocular disparity if the head is moved over a greater distance.

Head-movement parallax might be expected to be less effective than binocular parallax, because the disparate images are successive rather

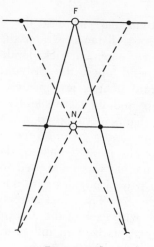

Figure 4.8

Crossed and uncrossed double images. If the eyes are fixated on N, F is seen on the right by the right eye and on the left by the left eye. If fixation is moved to F, N is seen on the left by the right eye and on the right by the left eye. (From Woodworth, R. S., Experimental Psychology, 1938. By permission of Holt, Rinehart and Winston, Inc.)

than simultaneous. The fact that the head is moved in the process also gives rise to *movement perspective* or *parallax*, which is itself a powerful cue of distance or depth: objects close to an observer in motion flow across the field of view faster than more distant objects do.

LIST OF CUES OF DEPTH

While the list of cues of depth that have been discussed so far is probably not exhaustive, it does sum to a substantial array.

CUES OF DEPTH REPRODUCIBLE IN PAINTINGS

Size
Partial overlap
Attached shadow
Cast shadow
Detail perspective
Aerial perspective through desaturation
Aerial perspective through addition of the ambient hue
Linear perspective
Color
Filled versus unfilled space
Blurring

MUSCULAR CUES OF DEPTH

Sensations of accommodation
Sensations of convergence

PARALLAX CUES OF DEPTH

Binocular parallax
 Seeing behind near objects
 Binocular disparity
 Crossed and uncrossed images
Movement perspective or parallax
Head-movement parallax

THE EXPERIMENTAL APPROACH

In this chapter, we shall present two examples of experimental analysis of the perception of depth, each representing a slightly different approach.

An analytical exploration of the phenomena associated with the difference between monocular and binocular vision is illustrated by the work of Panum (1858). He investigated a great many phenomena by constructing appropriate stimuli and observing the effect of binocular composition. He noted that when a stimulus containing a contour is presented to one eye, and a stimulus consisting of a homogeneous field is presented to the other, the contour is dominant. The dominance of contours over plain surfaces was stated by Panum as a law and is now a special case of figure-ground relationships.

When conflicting contours are presented to the two eyes, Panum noted binocular rivalry. Thus if a vertical line is presented to one eye and a horizontal line presented to the other, first one and then the other will be dominant, and the resolution of the two images into something resembling a plus symbol will be rare.

Some readers will be able to achieve binocular combinations of images by judicious crossing of the eyes. Figure 4.9 (and subsequent figures) can be used to illustrate Panum's principles by this method. Hold the book with the page at right angles to the line of sight and with the figures oriented on a line parallel to a line through the two eyes. Fixate the eyes on a point between the two figures, and then converge the eyes as if you are looking at a point about half way between your eyes and the book. Holding a pencil point in this vicinity and fixating on the point may help. Most people can achieve binocular fusion in this way, and their capacity to do so tends to improve with practice. If one is successful, Panum's principle of rivalry of contours will be immediately apparent; if one is unsuccessful, the demonstration kit contains a simple stereoscope that can be used to achieve binocular fusion.

Figure 4.9

*Binocular fusion of the two lines leads to rivalry of
contours at the point at which the lines overlap.*

Panum also noted that binocular perception might result in a
mosaic composition if the contours of the two images were not in conflict.
Thus the image of a bird presented to one eye and the image of a cage
presented to the other might well result in the perception of a bird *in*
the cage. Using the procedure suggested above, the reader may be able
to see the bird "in the cage" by binocular fusion of the two images in
Figure 4.10.

Figure 4.10

*Binocular fusion of the two images produces a "bird
in cage" mosaic without contour rivalry.*

The essence of binocular disparity as a cue of depth may be seen
by the reader who achieves fusion of each of the pairs of figures in
Figures 4.11, 4.12, and 4.13. It might not seem possible to combine
both *a* with *c* and *b* with *d* in Figure 4.11, but it is possible to do so.
The differences between the two images is about that of a ruler held
vertically between the two eyes and turned slightly, with one edge slightly
farther than the other from the observer. Figure 4.12 illustrates a relationship between size and shape constancy. If the two triangles are but two
views of the same triangle, it should be perceived in depth as turned
slightly on its vertical axis. Figure 4.13, when seen in depth, makes clear
that binocular disparity alone can produce simultaneous tilt in opposite
directions.

Figure 4.11

Simple binocular disparity. When fused binocularly, the perception is of a strip of material turned from the frontal plane.

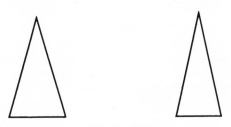

Figure 4.12

Binocular fusion of disparate triangles leads to perception of partial rotation of a single shape.

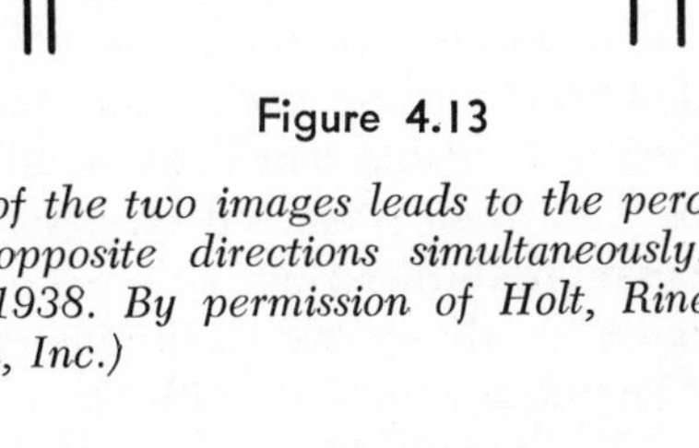

Figure 4.13

Fusion of the two images leads to the perception of tilt in opposite directions simultaneously. (Woodworth, 1938. By permission of Holt, Rinehart and Winston, Inc.)

If the reader has tried and succeeded in seeing depth in the accompanying figures, he may be aware that fusion of the disparate images is not always sufficient for the perception of depth. Often, fusion will occur; and the perception of depth occurs later, or may be attained, lost, and attained again. This common experience is a sufficient demonstration of the fact that binocular disparity is not, of itself, depth perception; it is a cue for the perception of depth.

Figure 4.14 can be used to illustrate a further point. Binocular disparity, as a cue of depth, is disparity in the horizontal plane. The eyes

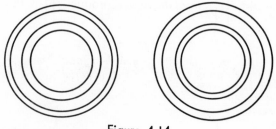

Figure 4.14

Two pairs of circles drawn in opposite disparity. The arrangement demonstrates the principle of prediction of the nature of the depth effect, and the difference between the effects of horizontal and vertical disparity. (Panum, 1858.)

can overcome slight vertical disparity, but the combined view does not yield any depth effect (Woodworth, 1938, p. 661). When depth is seen in Figure 4.14, the inner circle should be seen as tilted to the left and the outer circle tilted to the right. The same disparity in the vertical dimension does not produce an illusion of depth.

A modern experiment by Gibson (1950b) isolated a single cue of depth and determined the effect of quantitative variation in that cue. Gibson undertook to demonstrate the effectiveness of detail perspective, or the texture gradient, in producing the perception of *slant* independent of other cues of depth.

He produced stimuli by taking photographs of surfaces such as a brick wall, that had a uniform pattern, and other surfaces, such as unscreened gravel, that were homogeneous but contained irregular objects. Photos were taken at four different angles—10°, 22°, 30°, and 45°. Slides of these photos were then projected on a screen, with each slide projected in two orientations, either right side up or upside down.

Other possible cues of depth were eliminated, in the following manner, so that they would not interact with the cues from the texture gradient: (1) The stimuli were viewed monocularly to eliminate binocular disparity. (2) Head-movement parallax was eliminated by holding the head still. (3) Since the photograph was taken at an angle, but was projected on a vertical surface, accommodation was eliminated as a cue, as was the differential blurring which might have accompanied accommodation in natural viewing. Finally, (4) linear perspective was eliminated by having the subject view the stimuli through an aperture which covered the edges of objects which might have contributed to the perception of depth.

Gibson found that the texture gradient was a powerful cue of depth under these viewing conditions. As may be seen in Table 1, the observers were generally able to approximate a reproduction of the true slant of

TABLE I

Judged slant as a function of the gradient of texture density recorded in degrees of tactual-kinesthetic inclination to the vertical. Means of judgments by ten observers.

Texture	Physical Equivalent	Mean Judged Slant Upward Density Increase	Mean Judged Slant Downward Intensity Increase
Regular	10°	0.8°	8.5°
	22°	8.6°	15.9°
	30°	18.9°	21.9°
	45°	25.3°	28.6°
Irregular	10°	6.4°	8.6°
	22°	7.8°	7.7°
	30°	9.9°	9.2°
	45°	23.9°	17.9°

the objects by adjusting the slant of a board which was provided for the purpose. There was a tendency to underestimate the slant by about half. Accuracy was greater with the homogeneous than with the more irregular surfaces.

Without the necessity of performing a study in which many cues of depth are manipulated independently and in combination, Gibson's study demonstrates an important general point. While this chapter contains a long list of cues of depth, several, such as the texture gradient, will produce significant perception of depth when acting alone. The addition of more and more cues is likely to yield diminishing returns in achievement of a true depth effect. For this reason the painter need not make maximal use of all of the techniques at this command—a few well-executed ones are sufficient. It is no doubt a demanding task to remove every possible cue of depth in order to create the flat-appearing still life as seen in Braque's *Pink Tablecloth* (Plate IV).

(The demonstration kit contains a number of demonstrations which will serve to demonstrate Panum's principles, Wheatstone's arguments, and other effects. It also contains a number of demonstrations of illusions in size which have a direct effect on the perception of depth.)

The perception of an object seems to be relatively stable though the energy reaching the sense organs from that object changes. This phenomenon is called *object constancy*. For example, holding a circular piece of cardboard at arm's length and tilting it slowly produces the retinal image of a circle gradually changing to an ellipse. Under normal circumstances, the piece of cardboard is not perceived as changing shape; it remains a circle in experience (a tilting circle, to be sure). From a common-sense point of view this is the way things ought to look, and yet, why shouldn't the circle seem to change to an ellipse? The concepts to be discussed that are relevant to object constancy are basically simple. Two sets of distinctions between the physical world and one's experience of it should be kept in mind:

Distal stimulus versus proximal stimulus. The term *distal stimulus* refers to the physical energy of the stimulus at its source. The term *proximal stimulus* refers to physical energy as it impinges on the sense receptors. With respect to vision, the distal stimulus is light that is reflected or transmitted or emitted by an object. The energy must then traverse the distance between the object and the eye. It is scattered by air molecules, before it enters the eye. There it is refracted by the lens system, filtered through liquids and various retinal structures, and is finally brought to a focus, more or less, in the region of the receptors, near the back of the retina—that retinal image is the proximal stimulus. Both types of stimuli are of the real world, but it is important to distinguish between the energy affecting the sense organs and the energy at its source (the object).

Physical stimulus versus perceived stimulus. The term *physical stimulus* (objective stimulus) will be used as synonymous with the term distal stimulus. It is desirable, however, to contrast the characteristics of an object (the physical stimulus) with the *perceived stimulus* (subjective stimulus) that stands for the observer's experience of an object. The early psychological literature often failed to distinguish explicitly among distal, proximal and perceived stimuli. (One's experience of the world was presumed identical with the world itself.) The paradox of size and shape constancy arises when it is realized that the perceived stimulus tends to correspond not to the proximal stimulus upon which it is based but to the distal stimulus.

SIZE CONSTANCY

A good descriptive account of size constancy can be given, although there is theoretical controversy about the mechanisms involved. The extent or area (size) of the distal stimulus is the "tape-measured size," so to speak, of the physical stimulus "out there." The size of the proximal stimulus is that of the image focused on the retina.

The perceived size of an object seems to be relatively constant though the size of the proximal stimulus may vary widely with the distance from the object to the perceiver. This is size constancy. The perceived stimulus is of an object of constant size even though the perceiver must base his perception upon a proximal stimulus (retinal size) which is *not* constant as the distance from object to perceiver varies. Figure 5.1 presents the geometry of the situation, and

$$\frac{S}{D} = \frac{R}{K}, \text{ i.e., } K\frac{S}{D} = R.$$

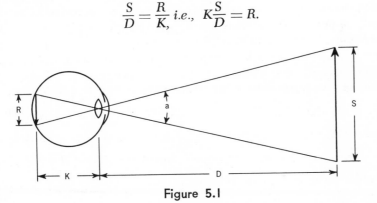

Figure 5.1

The geometry of retinal size.

The distance between the retina and the focal point of the eye (K) is approximately constant. Retinal size (R) is therefore directly related to physical size divided by physical distance. Angle a, the angle subtended by the object at the eye (termed visual angle), can be determined if S, physical size, and D, physical distance, are known. Retinal size R, depends upon angle a; if two objects subtend the same visual angle, the retinal sizes are identical. For example, doubling both S and D leaves a and R unchanged. Retinal size, R, by itself is insufficient to permit determination of S, the physical size of the object.

The perceived size of an object, then, depends upon two important pieces of information from the real world, the physical size of the object and the physical distance of the object from the observer; neither piece of information is directly provided the observer in the proximal stimulus. In addition to the proximal stimulus, however, the observer has a variety of information stored in memory (such as the relative sizes of familiar objects). With the assistance of this information, the observer can usually infer the size of the object and its distance away. Egon Brunswik (1955) has shown quite conclusively that people are very poor at estimating the size of retinal images but are good at estimating distal size.

One way to illuminate the nature of the problem involved in size constancy is to write two equations, one pertaining to the physical world and one pertaining to subjective experience. They are:

$$K\frac{S}{D} = R \quad \text{and} \quad k\frac{s}{d} = R.$$

The S and D in the equation on the left refer to physical dimensions. The s and d in the equation on the right refer to experienced size and distance.* Note that retinal size, R, appears in both equations. It seems reasonable that s should be influenced by altering d even though R remains the same. That is, with a given retinal size, perceived size should depend on perceived distance. Such a conclusion is easy to demonstrate. Experiment 10 in the demonstration kit provides a drawing of a corridor, giving the illusion of depth to a flat surface. If two objects identical in physical height are positioned in the corridor, the one "farther down the corridor" appears to be taller. Why? First, from the physical equation $K\frac{S}{D} = R$, S and D are the same. Therefore, the two objects produce images with identical retinal sizes. But the perspective drawing introduces differences in perceived depth. Since $k\frac{s}{d} = R$ and R is the same for each object, if d, perceived distance, increases then s, perceived size, does likewise.

Demonstration 11 in the demonstration kit is a somewhat more complicated illustration. Two normal-sized cards are used, one with a rectangular piece removed from a corner. The cards are aligned so that when they are viewed monocularly, the missing corner in the near card is exactly filled by a corner of the far card. That is, the uncut card appears to overlap the cut card and thus seems to be in front of it. Actually, the uncut card is farther away. As noted in the previous chapter, interposition is a cue for depth. We presumably have learned that if one object partially obscures another, then the object which is obscured is farther away. We also are familiar with the size of playing cards. The perceptual demonstration presents two conflicting depth cues, familiar size and inter-

---

* The equation for subjective experience ought to be written $s/d = f(R)$; i.e., the ratio of perceived size to perceived distance is a function of (depends upon) R. The possible nature of the relationship is an issue which will not be discussed. For the purpose of explaining size constancy, the simplified relationship can be employed.

position. Interposition wins out. The card with the corner removed is perceived as farther away; since it is physically closer, it is then perceived as larger. Why? Both playing cards are equal in physical size, S. But of the two cards, the one with the corner missing is closer, therefore producing a larger retinal size, R. Rearrange the terms of the formula to get $s = \dfrac{Rd}{k}$. R is larger for the card with the corner missing; and, because of false interposition, perceived distance, d, is also larger. The product, R times d, predicts a greater perceived size, s. If a diagram of the angles involved is drawn, the result should be practically self-evident.

A famous experiment by Holway and Boring (1941) shows unmistakably the influences of perceived size and distance. A subject was stationed at the intersection of two hallways and observed a circle of light (test circle) which was placed in one hallway. The experiment was designed so that as the test circle was moved down the hall, its size increased proportionally—keeping angle a, the visual angle, the same regardless of physical distance. Because visual angle never changed for any of the physical circles, retinal size, R, was also identical for all circles. Ten feet away in the other corridor was a comparison circle, and the subject's task was to set the size of the comparison circle to match the test circle as it was placed at different distances. The most obvious distance cues were eliminated. The objects were viewed with one eye, through a small opening, in a darkened corridor. Can you predict the outcome? (Refer to Figure 5.2.)

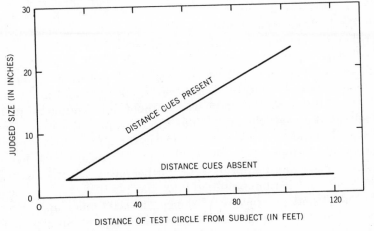

Figure 5.2

The relation of judged size to distance. (Based on the graph of Holway and Boring [1941] and reproduced by permission of The American Journal of Psychology.)

The subjects tended to produce the same setting of the comparison circle regardless of the physical distance of the test circle. The observer's only obvious cue was retinal size, which never changed. With other distance cues present and the observer permitted normal binocular vision, the comparison circle was adjusted very closely to the physical size of the test stimulus. Thus, when an observer has distance cues available, he tends to make accurate estimates of the real size of the object. When distance cues are reduced or absent, estimates tend to correspond with retinal sizes.

An interesting failure of size constancy is the moon illusion. When the moon is observed near the horizon, it appears approximately 1½ times larger than when it is high in the sky. The phenomenon is not due to atmospheric refraction, since photographs of the moon in any position yield images of just about the same diameter, proving that a retinal image, R, is nearly the same in all cases. Rather convincing experiments by Kaufman and Rock (1962) suggest that the illusion is due to a change in perceived distance, d. The explanation goes as follows: The moon looks bigger on the horizon because it is experienced as farther away; in the formula $k\frac{s}{d} = R$, since R is constant, an increase in d will produce an increase in s. (Note the similarities to the Holway and Boring study, where R is also constant.) Kaufman and Rock used an apparatus which, from the subject's point of view, projected an artificial moon into the real sky. With two artificial moons, one at the horizon and one at the zenith, diameters of the artificial moons could be adjusted until the two were perceived as equal. To make the zenith moon appear equal in size to the horizon moon, the zenith moon required a diameter 1.48 times larger than the horizon moon. If the terrain under the horizon moon were masked by having the subject observe through a hole in a sheet of cardboard, the illusion disappeared. By means of prisms and mirrors the horizon was moved up to the zenith moon, and a second moon was observed near the horizon but viewed without surrounding terrain. The illusion was reversed; the zenith moon now appeared larger. Thus the presence of terrain near the moon makes it appear larger regardless of the moon's position in the sky or the angle of regard. One hypothesis is that the moon must appear to be farther away when it is near the terrain. The explanation presumes that the physical size of the moon (2,160 miles) and its objective distance (239,000 miles approximately) are so great as to be incapable of registering accurately in experience. In contradiction to this hypothesis, if observers are asked why the moon on the horizon appears larger, they reply, "because the moon seems closer there." Perhaps people describe the moon as closer *because it looks bigger*.

A discussion of size constancy would not be complete without consideration of an interesting perceptual experience and Emmert's Law, with which it is associated. There are several ways to fix an image on the retina so that it outlasts the application of the stimulus for an appreciable length of time. One method is to produce either a positive or a negative afterimage. The demonstration kit contains several demonstrations (see Demonstrations 3 and 4). When a shape such as a white square on black surroundings is viewed while being illuminated with a bright flash of light, the result is usually an afterimage of a square. Under proper conditions, the image will endure for several minutes. The observer may then look at surfaces at different distances. The afterimage tends to have an "out there" appearance and to be superimposed upon the surface viewed. The size of the afterimage varies directly with the distance of the surface onto which it is "projected." If the observer looks at a near surface, the image will appear very small. If he looks at a far surface, the image will look very large. This is Emmert's Law.

It might be argued that Emmert's Law does not correspond to findings about size constancy. The common observation is that in contrast to the behavior of projected afterimages, objects, if they change size at all, seem to become smaller as they recede. But the law of size constancy is not contradicted. In the subjective-size formula, $k\dfrac{s}{d} = R$, subjects can utilize distance cues in a dim room; they therefore have information available for a determination of d. The retinal size, R, is a constant; the afterimage has been fixed upon the retina. Therefore, if d is perceived as increased, s should be perceived as larger also. The result is not at all surprising and is perfectly consistent with the statements about size constancy. Part of the confusion lies with the formulation of Emmert's Law. According to Edwards and Boring (1951), Emmert apparently did not distinguish between perceived size or distance, and physical size or distance. At any given physical distance of the projection surface, it has been shown that the tape-measured size of the projected afterimage fits the equation pertaining to the real world, $K\dfrac{S}{D} = R$. R is the fixed size of the positive afterimage. D is the objective distance to the projection surface. When the observer projects his afterimage on the surface and adjusts two spots of light (also on the surface) to bracket the afterimage, S (the distance between the spots) corresponds reasonably well to the formula. Whether or not distance cues are available to the observer is immaterial. It has not yet been shown that the perceived size of the positive afterimage will change without any change in objective distance, D, when an illusion misleads the observer as to the surface's "real" location. That is, given that tape-measured size is determined by the real-world equation, is the subject's estimate of the tape-measured size determined by the equation pertaining to the experienced world? One of the authors (D. J. W.) is in the process of performing such an experiment, and success seems virtually certain.

SHAPE CONSTANCY

Shape constancy refers to the experience of an object as retaining a rigid shape although the proximal stimulus, the retinal image, changes with a change in the viewing angle. At the beginning of the chapter, it was pointed out that a circle is still perceived as a circle even though it is tilted and the retinal image thus becomes elliptical. This phenomenon is an example of shape constancy. Shape constancy presents problems similar to those of size constancy. If cues are available which allow the observer to infer slant—a form of depth perception—then shape constancy can prevail. Tilting a square represents the far edge of the square as a shorter line in the retinal image; a tilted square leads to a trapezoidal proximal stimulus. If the surface is textured—with a sandpaper finish, for example—the texture gradient can serve as a cue. With depth cues absent, slant disappears perceptually, and a tilted square can be perceived as a trapezoid perpendicular to the line of sight.

Shape constancy applied to three-dimensional shapes. Objects are not perceived as becoming distorted or misshapen as the angle of regard changes. The Kopfermann cubes reproduced in Figure 5.3 (see also Experiment 34 in the demonstration kit) are a series of line drawings which can be perceived as different two-dimensional patterns. However, if these patterns are perceived tri-dimensionally, each appears to be a cube from a different angle of regard.

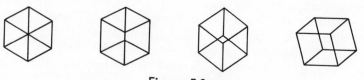

Figure 5.3

The Kopfermann cubes.

The constancies in the perception of size and shape have a biologically adaptive function. They permit one to perceive the world as relatively stable and unchanging. Try to imagine what the world would look like if the size and shape of everything appeared to correspond to the size and shape of the retinal image. We can assume that the world of shapes corresponds roughly to the way in which we perceive them.

Illusions in visual perception, as indicated previously, constitute an interesting class of events in which the perceived stimulus and the distal stimulus do not match. Illusions are of intrinsic interest; but more importantly, experimental work with illusions is beginning to lead to better understanding of the perceptual process on the one hand, and to data which are possibly relevant to cortical physiology on the other.

A series of illusions, including the Müller-Lyer illusion of Figure 6.1, is presented in Demonstrations 19 through 31 of the demonstration kit. Most of these illusions are well known to psychologists. Venerable names from the history of psychology are attached to many of them. The

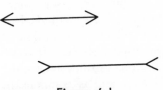

Figure 6.1

The Müller-Lyer illusion.

illusions are forcible reminders that perception does not necessarily tend toward veridicality—without question, one's surroundings influence what one perceives. Little is known about why illusions occur. Gestalt psychologists attempted to explain them in terms of force fields set up in the brain by the total configuration of the display. However, Sickles' (1942) work represents one of the very few attempts actually to apply the theory of a "field of forces."

Investigations have determined how much distortion is produced by the arrowheads in the Müller-Lyer illusion (Demonstration 19, Figure 6.1), and they have determined that, with practice, the illusory effect diminishes (Judd, 1902). Painstaking work by Künnapas (1955) with the so-called horizontal-vertical illusion (Figure 6.2) has shown that the illusion is the result of two influences: (1) Though both lines are objectively equal, the vertical line appears longer; this is truly a horizontal-vertical illusion. (2) A dividing-divided illusion also exists; the line which does the dividing appears longer. The double effect is revealed when one

45

Figure 6.2

The   horizontal-vertical   illusion.

places the vertical line at different locations along the horizontal line. The length illusion is at a maximum when the dividing line bisects the divided line, and diminishes progressively until, with an L-shaped arrangement, the illusion is minimal. Thus without the dividing-divided illusion there is a residual horizontal-vertical illusion. By rotating the display 90°, ⊣ , the two effects are opposed. The bisecting (but now horizontal) line still appears longer but to a lesser extent. And, using the rotated display, ⊣ , if the horizontal line is moved along the vertical line, a point is found where the two lines look equal in length; further movement makes the horizontal line appear shorter. It has been suggested that the inverted T display is perceived as tilted backward at the top as if it were a foreshortened vertical line, and is compensated for in experience to achieve constancy (see Chapter 5, Size and Shape Constancy).

When the vertical line is centered on the horizontal, Künnapas' data reveal that for both lines to appear equal in length, the ratio of length of vertical line to length of horizontal line is 0.869. Interestingly, the ratio of altitude to base of an equilateral triangle is 0.866. By connecting the endpoints of the horizontal-vertical illusion when its two lines appear to be equal in length, one gets an equilateral triangle! An equilateral triangle, by the standards of Gestalt theory, is a good figure. The correspondence of the above ratios might well represent something more than sheer coincidence.

FIGURAL AFTEREFFECTS

Line illusions exhibit various kinds of distortion—a change in location, length, or size, or an alteration in shape—i.e., a sort of simultaneous pattern contrast. One can produce what might be called successive pattern contrast by presenting first the features that produce distortion, followed after a short time by the rest of the figure. For example, in the Müller-Lyer illusion, presenting the arrowheads alone, followed by horizontal lines alone, gives the same type of length distortion. Such phenomena are called figural aftereffects, although it is not certain that the processes involved are much different from the ones for simultaneity of presentation.

Figural aftereffect is distortion or displacement of a perceived pattern as a result of the fixation of a previous pattern. Figural aftereffects (FAE) have received a great deal of emphasis, partly because Gestalt psychologists have considered them to be crucial confirmations of their field theory of perception.

(Two relevant experiments are included in the kit. One is Experiment 35, after Köhler and Wallach (1944), demonstrating the displacement of rectangles in a direction away from previously fixated rectangles. The other is Experiment 36, from J. J. Gibson (1933) dealing with the distortion of a straight line; an aftereffect bows it opposite to a curved line initially fixated upon.)

In accordance with the usual terminology, the figure initially fixated is called the inducing figure or I-figure. The time of this fixation is called inspection time. Then, after a delay (delay time may be zero), the test figure or T-figure follows. The amount of distortion or displacement of the T-figure from its "true" state can be measured in a variety of ways.

Let us illustrate figural aftereffects with concentric circles. Experiments are usually performed with a tachistoscope, an apparatus that

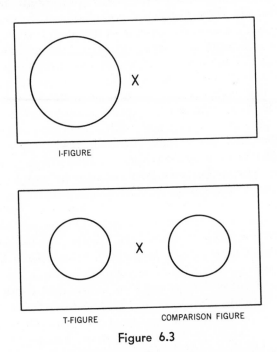

Figure 6.3

Cards used in determining figural aftereffects for concentric circles.

allows the experimenter to control inspection time and delay time. A slide projector with a timer-operated shutter can serve as a tachisto-scope. The subject fixates the "X" adjacent to the I-figure in Figure 6.3. After the required inspection time, the screen darkens, then T-figure and comparison figure appear. When the subject fixates the "X" between them, the T-figure is concentric with the previous stimulation from the I-figure. One straightforward method of measurement is to provide a comparison figure (presumably not much influenced by the previous I-figure, since it is on the other side of the fixation point), which can be adjusted by the subject until its size matches the apparent size of the T-figure. The amount of displacement, in this case a change in the perceived size of the T-circle, can be found by subtracting the true diameter of the T-circle from the diameter of the comparison circle when both were perceived as equal.

Kinesthetic aftereffects (KAE), involving the muscle senses, can be produced in similar fashion. The batter who swings several bats on his way to the plate, so that his single bat will seem lighter, is a real-life example of a kinesthetic aftereffect that results in an apparent change in weight. The most frequently studied KAE is the change in the experi-ence of width. Typically, the subject rubs a rectangular object of a given width (the I-block) between thumb and middle finger for a specified inspection time. He then grasps an object of a different width (the T-block). One can measure the amount of kinesthetic aftereffect by mov-ing the other hand along an elongated wedge (comparison block) until a point is reached where perceived width is equal for each hand. The objective width of the T-block is then subtracted from the width chosen on the comparison block, to find the amount of the aftereffect.

What kinds of experimental results occur with FAE and KAE? One might expect greater displacement with longer inspection time, and the data confirm this prediction (Hammer, 1949; Bakan, Myers, and Schoonard, 1962). One might also expect that the displacement continues to diminish, the longer the time delay between inspection and test and this is so (Hammer, 1949) in general, although at least one experimenter has reported an increase in displacement (Bakan *et al*, 1962). Displace-ment may take one of two forms, assimilation or contrast. Assimilation is displacement of the T-figure *toward* the I-figure, while contrast is dis-placement of the T-figure *away from* the I-figure. Generally FAE and KAE exhibit contrast, as do the concentric circles used here for illustra-tion and in the demonstrations provided in the demonstration kit. For example, if the T-figure is a circle smaller than the I-figure, the T-figure will be perceived as even smaller than it really is. Surprisingly, when two concentric circles are presented as a spatial illusion (simultaneously, as in Figure 6.4), the reverse effect, assimilation, occurs. The inner circle of the doughnut and the comparison circle are of the same objec-

COMPARISON CIRCLE

Figure 6.4

The Delboeuf illusion.

tive size. In this simultaneous form, the illusion is called the Delboeuf illusion.

One might expect that the smaller the distance between T-figure and I-figure, the greater the aftereffect. The findings are not that simple and lead to a result known as the distance paradox (Charles and Duncan, 1959; Sagara and Oyama, 1957). As the I-figure comes closer to the T-figure, the amount of displacement increases, but the maximum displacement occurs before T-figure and I-figure are coincident. As the distance decreases farther, toward zero, the amount of displacement also decreases toward zero. See Figure 6.5.

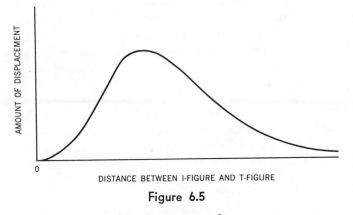

Figure 6.5

The distance paradox.

Although contrast is normally reported in KAE studies, one experimenter has reported that some subjects exhibit either contrast or assimilation in a very consistent fashion. Petrie (1960) has labeled one group of her subjects "Reducers" because they produce assimilation, shrinkage of the T-figure when it is wider than the I-figure, and contrast, shrinkage of the T-figure when it is narrower than the I-figure, thus tending to reduce the experienced width of the T-figure in both instances. Similarly, "Augmenters" tend to increase the perceived size of the T-figure regardless of the relative size of the I-figure. Tests have shown that "Augmenters" can bear forced isolation better than "Reducers" but are more disturbed by pain. The data make sense if one considers that "Augmenters" amplify experienced stimulation and "Reducers" diminish it. Petrie's findings are obviously important for the study of personality, and merit careful scrutiny and retesting by other investigators.

Gestalt psychologists have explained figural aftereffects by means of a satiation theory. As the outline of a circle (an I-figure) is fixated, an electrical field in the cortex which represents the circle is said to become "satiated" and tends to resist further excitation. The amount of satiation is considered to decrease progressively across the cortex away from "the locus of the circle." The cortical representation of the T-circle is detoured, so to speak, into a region of lesser satiation; the result is contrast, a change in perceived size. Satiation theory does not directly account for the distance paradox, since the theory seems to imply that the amount of displacement should continue to increase as the distance between I-figure and T-figure decreases. See Osgood (1953) for a more extended discussion of satiation theory and alternative explanations of the distance paradox. The neurophysiological aspects of satiation theory have been criticized primarily because of disagreement with the concept of a field of electrical forces in the cortex. A well-known experiment was performed by Lashley, Chow, and Semmes (1951). They showed no resulting defects in pattern vision when either gold strips were placed on or gold pins were inserted into the visual cortex of monkeys in an effort to "short-circuit" the electrical force fields.

Probably none of the explanations proposed thus far for FAE and KAE is adequate. In actuality, the evidence on which to base a theory is rather fragmentary. Such effects ought to provide an important means of investigating pattern perception, but as yet they seem to raise more questions than they answer.

ILLUSIONS IN THREE DIMENSIONS

Illusions occur in three dimensions as well as in two, and often result when two sets of visual information are placed in contradiction to each other. The distorted room developed by Adelbert Ames, Jr. (see Experiment 37 in the demonstration kit), is constructed in misleading perspective. When viewed with one eye from the proper position through the peephole, it appears to be a normal rectangular room. However, the left corner visible through the peephole is actually twice as tall as the right corner. The left corner is also twice as far away, the floor and ceiling are slanted appropriately, and the far wall actually recedes from right to left. All the rules for geometrical perspective are observed; the image on the retina therefore corresponds closely to that of a normal room, and it is perceived as normal. But if identical objects, placed one in each corner, are observed, the object in the right corner appears larger because it produces a larger retinal image. This occurs even if the identical objects are familiar, such as two pennies. Apparently, the observer tends to perceive stable surroundings in the face of conflicting information from the environment. In full-sized replicas of the distorted room a person will seem to change size as he walks from one corner to the other.

The trapezoidal window, also developed by Ames, is another powerful illusion (see Experiment 38 of the demonstration kit). The window is drawn in perspective, so that when observed at a right angle to its surface it appears to be a window seen on the slant. One vertical edge is smaller, and shadows are properly simulated. When the window is rotated through 360°, it appears to be oscillating back and forth through 180°, with the shorter vertical edge remaining farther away. Thus our past experience with windows seen from different angles provides a characteristic image on the retina leading to an illusion of false oscillation. When a rod is placed through the window and the window and rod allowed to rotate, the window appears to oscillate back and forth through 180°, but the rod appears to rotate through 360°, leading to the anomalous situation of a solid rod seemingly penetrating a solid window frame. An object attached to a corner of the window appears to float through space for half its 360° rotation when the window corner on which it is placed is perceived at a false distance. Allport and Pettigrew (1957) have reported that Zulus, whose culture is relatively lacking in rectangular shapes like windows, are not as subject to the illusion as are members of European cultures. If this is so, the effects of past experience are quite clear.

As was suggested at the beginning of the chapter, one may approach larger questions through an investigation of perceptual peculiarities. There is no doubt that the study of illusions has added to our understanding of perception. Good descriptive accounts can be given about many of the illusions, under what conditions they occur, and the magnitude of their effects. Theoretical explanations, however, remain a source of lively controversy.

THE STIMULUS FOR COLOR

The sun, light bulbs, television transmitters, x-ray machines—many energy sources emit electromagnetic radiation. Light is defined as visible electromagnetic radiation. Note that the definition includes not only the physical energy, radiation, but also the qualification that, to be classed as light, radiation must be within the range of human visual experience.

Energy reaching the eye may be characterized by its wavelength and intensity. The visible range of wavelengths runs approximately from 400 millimicrons to 750 millimicrons. When the amount of energy (intensity) is known at each wavelength, then the physical stimulus has been specified.

The term *color* applies to experiences (attributes) associated with light. Color has three attributes: *brightness,* roughly corresponding to the intensity of the light, plus two chromatic attributes, *hue* and *saturation.*

Color names, such as red and green, are hue designations. When a prism separates sunlight by wavelength, a spectrum of ordered colors results. Proceeding from short to long wavelengths are violet, indigo, blue, green, yellow, orange, and red, with each hue shading into the next. Single wavelengths have characteristic hues. However, when wavelengths are mixed, the resulting color need not appear to be composed of the hues of its components. Sunlight contains energy at all visible wavelengths, yet seems to be more or less white. One can understand why Sir Isaac Newton encountered difficulties in convincing his fellow scientists that sunlight consists of, and can be split into, components of such brilliant hue.

Saturation is related to the amount of white a color appears to contain; the less white, the higher the saturation. Single wavelengths from the spectrum have maximum saturation. One way to desaturate a color is to add white. For example, red plus white produces a desaturated red (pink). Since white light consists of a mixture of wavelengths, it would seem reasonable that mixing any wavelengths of different hue can never increase the saturation of the mixture, and such is the case. To repeat, saturation is related to the amount of white a color *appears* to contain. Colors with zero saturation—black, grays, and white—are termed achromatic colors, achromatic meaning without chromaticness (no hue and no saturation). Chromatic colors do possess hue and saturation.

COMPLEMENTARY COLORS

There are several ways to mix colors psychologically, with results quite different from the more familiar mixing of colored pigments. The demonstration kit contains material for producing color mixtures with a color wheel—a method of spinning colors rapidly enough so that they seem to fuse. The most dramatic effect of color mixing on the color wheel is, perhaps, the result of mixing two hues. If an appropriately chosen blue and yellow, in the proper proportions, are rotated, an achromatic gray is seen instead of the green that would probably result from the mixing of pigments. Two colors are said to be complementary when they can be mixed in some proportion to produce an achromatic experience. Blue and yellow therefore qualify as complementary colors. Every color has a complement.

THE COLOR CIRCLE AND THE COLOR SOLID

The color circle is an abstraction that can help to clarify some of the above statements by representing color attributes schematically. Let the hues be arranged in their rainbow order around the perimeter of a circle. Then let us ignore the physical world of wavelengths and plot

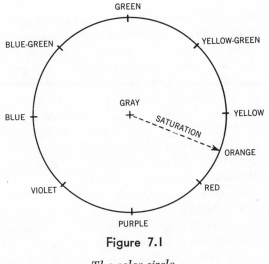

Figure 7.1

The color circle.

the psychological experiences—hues. In Figure 7.1, saturation is repre-sented as distance from the center, the center being the achromatic point. Complementary colors lie on opposite sides of the circle. Now imagine a third dimension to represent brightness, and we have the

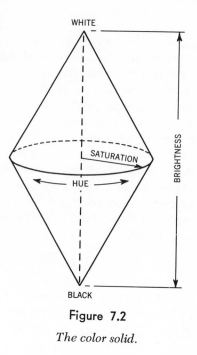

Figure 7.2

The color solid.

color solid (Figure 7.2). Any color can be specified as to hue, saturation, and brightness, occupying a place in, or on the surface of, the solid.

The most saturated colors that can be experienced lie on the surface of the solid; the less saturated colors lie in the interior; achromatic stimuli fall along the vertical centerline. If one uses numbered scales to indicate each of the three dimensions of the color solid, one has the beginnings of a psychological color-specification system. The Munsell Color System (Munsell Color Company, Baltimore, Maryland) is a notable, widely used example of this approach. Let us emphasize that the composition of the physical stimulus is being ignored. It is the *appearance* of the colors that is being plotted.

Is it possible, knowing the specifications of a physical stimulus, to predict the result in perception? The answer, in a large measure, is "Yes." One can predict the quantities of each of three internationally agreed-upon standard colors necessary to match perfectly the physical stimulus in question. Human subjects, mixing the hues of three standard lights, have matched the color of other samples, including single wavelengths from the spectrum, that permit us to predict how people with normal color vision will match any possible physical stimulus. The details of the color-prediction process are beyond the scope of this volume, but one important fact on which such predictions are based must be stated explicitly. Colors produced by different wavelength compositions can appear identical to the eye. Colors that look identical but differ in physical composition are called *metameric pairs*. Such pairs demonstrate that the perceptual system cannot discriminate the component wavelengths that comprise a color—this is at the root of our inability to give a simple physical analog for hue and saturation. For example, complementary colors, when mixed, produce gray. Different pairs of complementary colors can form an identical gray. These two grays constitute a metameric pair, and an observer cannot tell visually which gray results from which set of complementaries.

The discussion so far has considered only additive color mixtures, such as those formed by use of the color wheel or by superimposing projected lights on a high-quality reflecting screen. In effect, the reflected light is an additive combination of the incident lights. If two lights look identical (are a metameric pair), they can be substituted for each other in an additive color mixture. That is, colors that look alike act alike in an additive color mixture, and one need not concern himself with the exact composition of the electromagnetic radiation. Furthermore, the outcome of an additive color mixture can be predicted on the basis of the appearance of the components.

Passing white light through two superimposed chromatic filters yields an example of a subtractive color mixture. When white light reaches a filter, certain wavelengths are absorbed, others are transmitted —the transmitted light reaching the eye determines the hue of a filter. (Many red filters transmit only radiation in the long-wavelengths end of the visible spectrum and absorb all other wavelengths.) When two filters are superimposed, light is transmitted only if both filters transmit wavelengths in common. The rest of the light is absorbed (subtracted). In order to predict the outcome of a subtractive color mixture, the characteristic hues of the filters as seen in white light do not provide enough information. The type of light source must be known, as well as the transmission characteristics of the filters at each visible wavelength.

Here is an example of the way additive and subtractive color mixtures differ: In additive color mixtures, yellow and blue in proper proportions make gray. One need not know the physical make-up of either hue. In a subtractive color mixture, when yellow and blue are mixed (using filters, for example), the result may be green. The yellow filter transmits wavelengths with a yellow characteristic hue, transmits a reduced amount of green wavelengths, and absorbs blue wavelengths. The blue filter transmits blue, transmits some green, and absorbs yellow. Together, the two filters transmit mostly green wavelengths. By contrast, special filters have been developed which transmit essentially a single wavelength and absorb all others (monochromatic filters). If yellow and blue monochromatic filters are superimposed, the mixture is not green. No light will be transmitted; the result is a black. The demonstration kit

(Experiments 1 and 2) contain materials for demonstrating additive and subtractive color mixtures.

With the many different dyes and pigments available, it is somewhat surprising that we are usually not too far wrong in our guesses about the resultant hue of a subtractive color mixture. You probably have learned that yellow paint mixed with blue paint gives green paint. (When paints are mixed, the process is partially one of subtractive color mixing, complicated by other factors such as internal scattering in the paint layer.) But there are no hard and fast rules for the subtractive mixing of hues. Subtractive mixing depends on the physical characteristics of the component stimuli, and the hues of the components are not sufficient to enable a correct prediction of every mixture. Our brief treatment of color has been presented in order that topics falling more closely under the heading of perception can be discussed properly. Color terminology and a certain familiarity with the physical stimulus for vision are necessary. For further details, the reader is referred to the vision chapter in Alpern, Lawrence, and Wolsk, *Sensory Processes*, in this series.

BRIGHTNESS CONSTANCY

The curtain is about to rise; as the house lights dim, the audience experiences a reduction in brightness. The electromagnetic energy proceeding from an object toward the eye has a specifiable intensity; the experienced intensity is called brightness. Brightness differences among shades of black, gray, and white will be considered. Objects are visible because they emit, transmit, or reflect light. A stable light source emits light at a characteristic intensity, but other objects can only transmit or reflect the light that reaches them. Most objects are visible because of reflected light, and therefore they have no characteristic intensity of their own. Observers attribute characteristic intensities to objects (this is brightness constancy), although the light intensity from most objects varies widely. Coal is said to be black and typewriter paper white. Coal in bright sunlight reflects more light than typewriter paper in moonlight; yet these viewing conditions do not make coal appear white or typewriter paper black. The perceiver does not act as a device that measures electromagnetic energy received from objects and converts it directly to brightness.

The difference between the characteristics of the perceived stimulus and the characteristics of the distal stimulus depends somewhat upon pupil contraction and expansion, which regulate the amount of light in the proximal stimulus, and upon the change in sensitivity of the light-sensitive pigments in the retinal receptors (dark and light adaptation). Both factors lead to a discrepancy between proximal and distal stimulus. (Perceived, proximal, and distal stimuli are discussed in Chapter V.) But pupillary and adaptation changes are relatively minor considerations in explaining discrepancies between the perceived stimulus and the distal stimulus. Experimental evidence shows that observers, under most circumstances, are sensitive not to the energy proceeding from an object but to that energy relative to the general level of illumination. That is, the crucial variable is not absolute intensity but relative intensity— the ratio between the intensity of the light from the object and the intensity of the light from the background. So, although brightness might seem to be related to the absolute intensity of the light from illuminated objects, it is more closely related to the percentage of incident (incoming) light reflected by an object. In sunlight, coal reflects more light than it does in moonlight, but the percentage of the illumination reflected is relatively constant. Percent reflectance, a property of objects, is called *albedo*. The quality of visual experience associated with albedo accounts in part for the brightness constancy that permits us to see coal as black, and white paper as white, over a wide range of illumination intensities. In everyday situations, the background illumination is not uniform, but subjects do utilize the retinal cues provided by the light intensity from objects, backgrounds, shadows, etc. An object may be shadowed by another. A perceptual cue for shadow is the *penumbra*, or partial shadow, surrounding the *umbra*, or main shadow. (See Experiment 9 in the demonstration kit.) Casting the shadow of a pencil on a piece of paper leads to the perception of shadow. However, if the penumbra is masked by a heavy black line, the shadowed area is experienced as a dimmer expanse of paper and not as shadow.

The shaded side of an object, such as a cube, is not perceived as less bright than the side in direct light. An object may even appear to emit its own light (i.e., be luminous) if it sends a great deal more energy to the eye than is provided by the general illumination. (In the second half of Experiment 9 in the demonstration kit, the bright spot, with penumbra masked, may appear to glow.)

Though the environment presents a mottled array of intensity levels as the observer's eye moves about the scene, he comes to some subjective decision about the state of illumination and perceives accordingly. In order to deceive the observer, one can provide false cues to the nature and direction of illumination, adding extra concealed light to surfaces, altering or hiding shadows, etc.

A dramatic experiment has been carried out by Gelb (see Woodworth and Schlosberg, 1954, pp. 441–442). He presented objects to an observer in a dimly illuminated room. A low-reflectance, and thus black, disc was illuminated separately by a concealed spotlight. The shadow cast by the disc was out of the observer's field of view. The black disc was perceived as "white" until a piece of high-reflectance, and thus white, paper was inserted to obscure part of the disc. The disc then appeared black. When the white paper was removed, the disc again appeared "white," even though the observer knew (at least intellectually) that it was black paper under added illumination. Apparently, knowledge of the state of affairs is not enough; the extra illumination must be evident in the retinal image.

COLOR CONSTANCY

In the previous section, brightness constancy was discussed only with respect to achromatic colors, but the concept of brightness constancy applies equally well to the brightness of colors possessing hue and saturation. Color constancy, on the other hand, refers to the principle that objects appear to retain nearly the same hue and saturation under different illuminating conditions. The term *chromatic constancy* is a more appropriate label, but one not generally employed.

Since most objects are visible because of reflected light, they have no characteristic energy proceeding from them and, strictly speaking, no color of their own. Perhaps you have had the experience of purchasing clothing in a shop equipped with fluorescent lights, only to find out later that, in sunlight or incandescent illumination, the color is different and possibly not at all to your liking.

As a reflecting object is seen under illuminations of different spectral compositions, the color of the object might be expected to change because the spectral composition of the light reflected from the object is different. However, with familiar objects under normal circumstances, color constancy prevails, and we tend to perceive very little change in hue or saturation. An experiment by Duncker (1939) illustrates the influence of color constancy. From the same sheet of green material, the silhouette of a leaf and the silhouette of a donkey were cut. Each was mounted on a white background, and the entire display was illuminated with red light, so that in the absence of color constancy the green material would be perceived as gray. Subjects matching the color of each object by means of disc colorimetry (see Experiment 1 of the demonstration kit), generally indicated that more green was required to match the leaf than the donkey. Although both objects were from the same material, and illuminated identically, the leaf was perceived as more toward green, the donkey as more toward gray. One might say that people know that donkeys are usually gray and leaves are usually green. Past learning produced a tendency toward color constancy. A breakdown of color constancy can be induced by withholding information or by providing false information. The experimenter can present unfamiliar objects, such as patches of paper, under abnormal illuminating conditions, so that the observer has no idea of characteristic color under normal daylight. The experimenter also can conceal the nature of the illumination from the observer.

It might be said that the characteristic color of a reflecting object is its color under normal conditions of viewing. But even the illumination outdoors is not the same on summer days and winter days, on clear days and cloudy days, at noon and at twilight. Thus, characteristic color, or color constancy, is a construction of the perceiver. A stable color is not really a property of reflecting objects, but usually we can act as if it were—we add stability to a changing environment.

Perfect constancy and complete lack of constancy are two extremes. With normal cues available, an observer approaches perfect constancy. Constancy can be reduced if environmental information is reduced; the subject will show lack of constancy if he is forced to rely on a bare distal stimulus devoid of the usual auxiliary cues. Also, he can be misled by false information. However, he is surprisingly good under everyday conditions. It must be remembered that the experience of constancy does not occur in a vacuum; other perceived changes accompany constancy. Thus when the proximal stimulus is shrinking, there are other cues that lead us to perceive the object not as shrinking, but as moving farther away.

The experience of color is a subjective phenomenon. It is sometimes said that color is a property of perception and not a property of distal stimuli. Many people would object to such an extreme statement, but it cannot be denied that the relationship between the experience of color and the nature of the distal stimulus is not nearly so simple as one would suppose without critical investigation. It is the purpose of this chapter to explore some of these complex relationships.

Given a normal human observer, it is possible, within certain limits, to predict, from a knowledge of the amounts of each wavelength of electromagnetic energy composing the light, the perceptual result of presenting light energy to the eye. The predictions are possible because normal observers have actually made color matches between a sample color and a comparison color composed of measurable amounts of three primary colors. The data from these observers become the standards on which predictions are based.

The science of color specification is called *colorimetry*. However, colorimetric matches are made under highly controlled conditions, usually in dark surroundings, using small patches of light as stimuli. Colorimetric predictions fail under great variety of circumstances. These deviations from colorimetric predictions are called—by tradition—"subjective colors." The term is mildly misleading to the extent that it implies that while making colorimetric measurements, the observer is being quite objective—acting like a well-calibrated machine; attending to and responding to the real physical stimulus. (Under everyday circumstances his color experiences are somewhat less mechanical.) A second implication is that these deviations from colorimetric predictions are unlawful and unpredictable. (Certain color experiences are just as "real" and probably more "natural" than the rigidly controlled experiences under the highly restricted viewing conditions of colorimetric measurement.) But in a sense, colorimetry provides standard data, based solely upon considerations of the amount of energy at each wavelength comprising the physical stimulus. The perception of color is based upon a host of other conditions found in the everyday world—which are eliminated in colorimetry—but are nonetheless of major importance.

A variable of prime importance in color perception is our past experience, both with familiar objects and with the effects of illumination. Such experiences play a role in color constancy which was discussed in the last chapter.

A second variable is the effect of alternating achromatic (black, gray, or white) light. The alternation of lights can be produced in various ways, (1) by flickering a stationary light off and on, (2) by looking at a light through a rotating disc with sectors removed (like looking through a rotating fan) so that the light source appears to be flickering, or (3) by spinning a cardboard disc—the disc being painted in an achromatic pattern. The laws of colorimetry predict that any additive mixture composed of some combination of black, gray, or white can mix to form only another achromatic black, gray, or white stimulus. These colorimetric predictions can be tested by means of the color wheel provided in Experiment 1, Disc Colorimetry, in the demonstration kit. However, if the alternation is performed somewhat below the critical flicker frequency (that is, below the point where the flickering stimulus is perceived as fused into a solid expanse of gray), the result is sometimes the perception of hues that, in the colorimetric sense, "should not be there." Such colors, usually somewhat desaturated (washed out), can even be perceived in a close pattern of lines, where it is assumed that small eye movements constantly alter the light reaching each color receptor. Pastel colors can be seen cutting across the lines of the

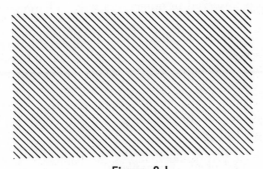

Figure 8.1

Inducing hue by means of parallel lines.

diagram in Figure 8.1. You may have observed a television commercial which proclaims that color can be perceived on your black and white television receiver; it was produced by a black and white border flickering at the proper speed.

Benham's Top, Figure 8.2, if rotated at a slow speed, will also produce the colors (Experiment 1 in the demonstration kit). The thin, black, curved lines appear as desaturated hues when the top rotates slowly. The position of the colors changes if the direction of rotation reverses.

Figure 8.2

Benham's top.

Even if the top is observed in other than white illumination, colors tend to appear.

Although the effects of flicker had been reported more than 100 years ago, why the hues are perceived is still an open question. The most probable explanation is based on the theory of the differential rise and fall of activity in the color receptors. It assumes that the color receptors of the eye, the cones, are not all equally sensitive to all wavelengths of light, and that they commence firing at slightly different times, though they are stimulated at precisely the same instant, and they cease firing at slightly different times when stimulation ceases. White light, of course, is normally composed of many wavelengths, and it is presumed that all the different varieties of color receptors are excited concurrently when white or gray is presented. When the alternation rate is appropriate, one type of receptor always fires slightly in advance of another, allowing the hue associated with that type of receptor to be perceived. Similarly, the experience could result if one type of receptor persists in its firing longer than another. That is, the color experience will result when the flicker rate is appropriate to allow one receptor type to fire in advance of or longer than other receptor types, leading to the perception of a particular hue rather than white.

If an adjustable-speed electric fan is available, one can peer in the direction of a bright light through the rotating blades. (Do not injure your eyes by using too intense a light source.) If the speed of rotation is adjusted properly, a myriad of flickering colors can be perceived. You may also perceive a pattern of hexagonally shaped colored cells, which is as yet a completely unexplained phenomenon. For some reason, such experience is sometimes emotionally upsetting, if prolonged. It may have dire consequences if the pilot of a private plane is flying his single-engine craft toward a sun which appears in front of his rotating propeller. The cure is to alter course or at least change the propeller rpm until the effect disappears. An interesting history and analysis of hue produced by flicker may be found in an article by Cohen and Gordon (1949), where many illustrations of black and white circular designs suitable for producing chromatic colors are presented.

Another form of subjective colors is based upon the effects of light which has preceded a stimulus in time (temporal effects), or light which surrounds the color in question (areal effects). Four phenomena are involved. They will be discussed in terms of chromatic effects (primarily hue). However, the descriptions hold for achromatic colors as well, where the changes are confined to alterations in brightness, as in Demonstration 3 in the demonstration kit, which is concerned with simultaneous and successive brightness contrast.

Positive afterimages. A brief, fairly intense flash of light leaves an aftersensation which is called a positive afterimage because it initially has the same color characteristics as the original flash. Perhaps you have experienced the aftereffects of a photo flash bulb. Images may persist for several minutes. A flash that is too intense or too long can result in permanent damage to the eyes. Afterimages exhibit peculiar characteristics. They can exist in the absence of any light; that is, a positive afterimage can be perceived in total darkness. It can be re-elicited after it has disappeared if the level of the room illumination is altered, and fairly intense positive afterimages seem to change hue over time as they fade. These hue shifts have been called the flight of colors. An afterimage will appear to be projected upon a surface in the field of view, and the size of the apparent image increases if the projection surface is moved farther away. This phenomenon is described by Emmert's Law, discussed in the chapter on size constancy. Positive afterimages are not very well explained, but it seems reasonable that they depend upon effects produced as retinal receptors recover from the initial flash of light. (See Chapter 2 of Alpern, Lawrence, and Wolsk, *Sensory Processes*, in this series.)

Chromatic adaptation (see Experiment 6 in the demonstration kit). The eye, as it moves freely about, adapts to the average illumination. We are always chromatically adapted to some level, to objects in view, and to the prevailing light sources in the environment. The general level of adaptation influences what we perceive. Colorimetry has become interested in the problems of predicting perceived colors under different states of adaptation. With extreme chromatic adaptation, startling effects have been found. Observers were placed in a room with "gray" walls illuminated by intense long-wavelength (red) light and allowed to adapt for 15 minutes. Then they were asked to judge the color of achromatic samples (a series of gray papers). Since the samples had never been presented in normal illumination, where they would have appeared as different shades of gray, observers were not influenced toward color constancy. When the samples were placed in the long-wavelength light, each sample could reflect only the red light, and thus, from colorimetry, it would be predicted that all the samples would appear red. The results showed that any "gray" sample that was lighter (had more reflectance) than the walls of the room did appear red. The sample that was the same as the walls appeared gray. Samples darker (with less reflectance) than the walls appeared blue-green, the complementary color to red, even though there were no blue-green wavelengths of light energy in the illumination. This experiment, performed by Helson in 1938, is one of the experiments on which Helson's Adaptation Level Theory is based.

Complete chromatic adaptation, the apparent absence of hue, in the presence of monochromatic light, can be obtained by means of a "Ganzfeld" (viewing conditions that produce a homogeneous expanse of light devoid of pattern). (See Experiment 7, the Ganzfeld, in the demonstration kit.) One simple method of producing a Ganzfeld is to tape a halved ping-pong ball over the eye, as a translucent eyecap. No matter where the eye moves, the view is the same. If chromatic light is then projected onto the eyecap, its hue gradually begins to fade toward gray, and for many subjects the experience of light disappears altogether after several minutes. Subjects have been reported to ask who turned off the lights (Hochberg, Triebel, and Seaman, 1951). Thus a continuous, uniform, chromatic source can be said to have failed as a stimulus; it was no longer being perceived. The conclusion merits emphasis. The mere presence of light is not sufficient for seeing; rather, stimulus change is necessary for a visual experience. The Ganzfeld creates a formless, depthless, unchanging visual experience, and in many instances observers have reported bizarre hallucinations while under Ganzfeld conditions for an extended period of time.

Successive color contrast (negative afterimages—see Experiment 4 in the *Perceptual Demonstration Kit*). When the eye fixates a chromatic stimulus and then moves on, the perception of succeeding stimuli tends to be modified by a hue complementary to the first. To produce a strong, fairly durable afterimage, fixate a colored square of paper for a minute; then switch your gaze to a gray surface. If the colored square was red, the afterimage is likely to be blue-green. If, instead of gray, one "projects" the afterimage onto a chromatic surface, its hue will tend to mix additively with the hue of the surface. With brief fixations the effects are more fleeting.

Simultaneous color contrast (see Experiment 5 in the demonstration kit). Simultaneous color contrast is a more or less instantaneous condition in which a surrounding hue tends to "induce" a complementary hue in the adjacent color. If one hangs gray drapes in a room painted in yellow, the drapes will tend to appear to have a blue cast. In order to achieve gray-appearing drapes they must be tinged with yellow which "mixes" with the blue of the simultaneous contrast hue to produce the experience of gray.

By means of either simultaneous or successive contrast, it is possible to achieve supersaturated hue experiences. Supersaturated hues appear even more saturated than the maximum saturation that can be achieved with monochromatic light from the visible spectrum. For example, if one fixates for a few moments on a spot of monochromatic blue-green and then views a large expanse of monochromatic red that is the exact complement of the blue-green, the additive mixture of the red afterimage and the red-illuminated surface will produce supersaturation.

Note that chromatic adaptation and successive color contrast are processes dependent on time. Chromatic adaptation can be considered a special case of overlapping successive contrasts. That is, each eye movement leaves a brief negative afterimage. The cumulative effect is a general influence of the over-all illumination affecting the adaptation of the retinal receptors.

Simultaneous color contrast is relatively independent of time, appearing practically instantaneously. Experiments in the laboratory support the contention that as long as "real" colors (i.e., those predictable from colorimetric measurements) can be identified when a scene is presented for a fraction of a second to an observer, the simultaneous contrast colors are also still identifiable. Are these subjective colors merely pigments of the imagination? (The authors cannot claim this pun. Jozef Cohen has employed it for many years in his lectures on color; he places its origin with the late Gordon Walls.) We are inclined to believe that most subjective color phenomena are independent of learning and are the direct result of a physiological reaction by the visual system to stimulation by light energy. For example, the prevalence of a color *complementary* to the physical stimulation in many color experiments is probably not sheer coincidence. Further, physiological recordings from various locations in the visual systems of animals demonstrate that certain nerve fibers which fire when a green light is *turned on* fire in exactly the same manner when a red light is *turned off*. For one of several possible illustrations of these findings, see DeValois's (1960) work with monkeys. Such evidence implies that the experience of a complementary blue-green afterimage, following a red adapting light, is identical physiologically to a "real" blue-green, since the nerve impulses are identical.

Indeed, within the past decade, the amount of agreement between psychological findings on subjective color and physiological studies of the functioning of color receptors and associated nerve pathways has become impressive.

A striking example of subjective colors was popularized by E. H. Land (1959). A camera, set on a tripod, takes two black and white photographic slides of the same scene. One picture is taken with a red filter in front of the camera lens. The other picture is taken with a green filter in front of the camera lens. The finished black and white photographic transparencies (positives) are identical with respect to the outline of objects, but due to the different light-transmittance characteristics of the two colored filters, identical objects appear in a different shade of gray on each transparency. Each black and white transparency is placed in an individual slide projector and projected through the same filter through which it was taken. The two resulting images are superimposed on the screen to form a single image and the green filter is removed. The scene is perceived in "full color." This result is surprising because it does not conform to colorimetric predictions. Both transparencies are black and white. One image is projected with red light, and the other with white light. The mixture of red and white light can be nothing other than shades of red from a highly saturated red, through pink, to an unsaturated white. Nonetheless, green, yellow, blue—in fact, "full color"— is reported, and the colors match the scene originally photographed fairly well. Red is the only hue which "ought to be seen," and if the surrounding areas are blocked off by looking through a tube (reduction screen) at a single area, the induced hue is reduced to a "shade of red." It appears, then, that simultaneous color contrast is involved, but simultaneous contrast ought only to produce colors complementary to red, that is, blue-greens. Chromatic adaptation to red undoubtedly occurs, since the screen is bathed in red light, causing the red component to appear faded. Color constancy is also involved. The "full color" is much more impressive when a large display of familiar objects is photographed than when a board containing color patches is photographed. We have learned that bananas and lemons are yellow; tree-ripened oranges are orange; apples are red.

The Land demonstrations have reawakened interest in subjective color phenomena because the demonstrations provided by light from a projector are much more striking than the effects found with traditional colored papers. If you are a camera enthusiast, reproducing the Land demonstrations is rather easy. However, do not be disappointed if the yellows and blues in your "full-color" reproduction do not turn out well; these hues are very difficult to achieve, requiring good contrast with fine gradations of density on the film.

E. H. Land has proposed a theory of color vision to account for his results. The theory differs considerably from the traditional theories concerned with color vision. There are indeed some puzzling aspects to the Land demonstrations, like the appearance of yellows and blues, but the majority of experimental findings can be explained with reference to subjective color phenomena. The color-specification system derived from colorimetric measurements cannot predict Land's colors because the conditions necessary for the occurrence of the colors are excluded during colorimetric measurements. However, current physiological work on the mechanisms of color vision is beginning to provide a basis for understanding why the effects occur in experience. (For a statement of Land's theory, see Land [1959]. There are also two strong rebuttals, both quite technical: one by Walls [1960] and the other by Judd [1960].)

Binocular color (see Experiment 8 in the demonstration kit). What occurs if a different hue is presented to each eye? Two possible results have been reported: fusion and rivalry. The hues may fuse into a single color experience. In the majority of instances, rivalry occurs—first one hue predominates, then the other, and the alternation process tends to continue. The perceptual result is of interest to color theorists, since colorimetry has determined that only three colors (and by inference, three color receptors in the eye) are sufficient to specify all colors. Some theorists have supposed that of the three types of color receptors in the eye, one is most responsive to red, one to green, and one to blue. A reason for this idea is that red, green, and blue are psychologically unique. That is, they do not seem in ordinary experience to be mixtures of other colors. Purple seems to be a mixture of red and blue, orange appears to be a mixture of red and yellow, and chartreuse seems to be a mixture of green and yellow, even when each of these hues is the result of monochromatic stimulation.

Yellow also has the quality of psychological uniqueness (it does not seem to be a mixture of other colors), but it is not one of the unique colors usually related to a receptor type. It is tempting to assign unique color experiences to instances where only one type of color receptor is being stimulated. Yet a hypothetical red-green-blue set of retinal receptors requires that yellow be signaled when both red and green receptors are responding. However, if an experience of yellow results from stimulating one eye with red and the other eye with green, then the experience of yellow might always be a cortical rather than a retinal phenomenon. If it is not retinal, than a red-blue-green color theory could be supported with greater assurance. This is an experiment in which even the facts are subject to some controversy. Some investigators have reported that when one eye is stimulated with red and the other with green, an experience of yellow results. A more common finding is that binocular color rivalry occurs with possible fleeting experiences of fusion into yellow. The demonstration kit affords an opportunity to try the experiment by use of appropriate filters. If one looks at a white surface with a green filter over one eye and red filter over the other, the conditions of test will be met. The experience is interesting and difficult to describe. Not everyone seems to achieve the same results.

The phenomena of subjective color illustrate the extent to which human perception involves a complex reconstruction of the world. They conflict with the idea that we simply see the world "as it really is."

The primary concern of this book has been with visual perception. Our neglect of other perceptual channels is not meant to imply that nothing is known about the perceiving processes of the other senses. Vision provides perhaps the richest source of information about the environment, and it has been the sense most widely investigated, but each sense presents unique problems. The interaction of the visual and vestibular senses will be considered in order to introduce the complexities of another sense and the vast possibilities for interaction among sensory systems.

The vestibular organs are a set of receptors in the semicircular canals and vestibular sacs located within the skull. They form a part of each inner ear structure, though not involved with hearing. The structure and function of the vestibular organs are treated in *Sensory Processes* by Alpern, Lawrence, and Wolsk. The receptors and associated nerve fibers are involved in the appreciation of bodily orientation with respect to gravity, in maintaining one's balance, and in experiencing acceleration and deceleration. Stimulating the semicircular canals excessively by a rapid increase or decrease in bodily rotation can lead to dizziness, nausea, pallor, sweating, and other symptoms common to motion sickness, but to no particular "sensations" which one might label as a characteristically vestibular experience. Certain forms of inner-ear defects are associated not only with deafness but also with vestibular malfunctions. Motion-sickness symptoms are absent from people with such defects even under the most severe experimental conditions. When blindfolded, such subjects have little idea of body position or motion, and it has been said that they dare not swim deeply underwater for fear of losing orientation with respect to the surface.

PERCEPTION OF THE HORIZONTAL AND THE VERTICAL

In normal humans, both vision and the vestibular senses are involved in the perception of the horizontal and the vertical. In aviation, it has long been known that some sort of visual reference for the horizontal with respect to the earth's surface is necessary—that "flying by the seat of the pants" (using the vestibular cues for maintaining orientation when in clouds or complete darkness) will guarantee a short life span. An alarmingly high number of private-aircraft accidents are attributable to improper procedure after loss of visual reference for the horizontal. Modern aviation is dependent upon instruments in the cockpit which can provide an artificial visual reference. The strong inclination to disbelieve his turn-and-bank indicator, or gyro (artificial) horizon, must be carefully trained out of the pilot. Demands made upon humans during space exploration have further increased interest in the perception of bodily orientation and of motion. Humans have been, and will be, subjected to unusual sense experiences, and their lives depend on how they perceive and react. For example, since the rotation of space platforms is being considered as a means to introduce artificial gravity forces, research is in progress to assess the effects of prolonged rotation upon human perception.

In general, it may be stated that normal earthbound observers are most strongly influenced by *visual* references to the environment with respect to perception of the vertical and horizontal. Under the usual visual circumstances, observers are influenced to a lesser extent by vestibular cues. If the visual frame of reference is eliminated (as in darkness), vestibular cues become dominant. With all visual cues absent, observers are exceedingly accurate in their estimate of the vertical, so long as they are not tilted. Subjects seated upright or standing erect in a completely dark room can adjust a dim luminous rod to vertical (in regard to gravity), with errors averaging at most about 2°. Experiments by Werner and Wapner (1952) indicate that when the left or right side of the body is stimulated, vertical settings are affected. Extraneous lights off to one side of the body will alter subjects' settings of a luminous rod to vertical in a predictable manner. In other words, a subject's *apparent* vertical is changed. The apparent vertical can also be disturbed when the observer is tilted, thus adding distortion by means of vestibular cues. Sensory-tonic theory assumes a stable state called *body equilibrium*, which is directly measurable by the setting of a rod to vertical. If vertical settings are altered, an alteration in body equilibrium can be measured, and the effect of environmental stimulation can be assessed. Werner and Wapner have shown that nonsymmetrical "extraneous stimuli"—electrical stimulation, for example—result in a shift of the apparent vertical toward the side opposite the nonsymmetrical stimulation. However, "object stimuli," such as the starting position of the luminous rod which is to be set to vertical, shift the apparent vertical toward the same side as the nonsymmetric stimulation. Object versus extraneous stimulation is a concept similar to the figure-ground distinction made by Gestalt theory, except that "ground" need not be visual background but might be any background stimulation from vestibular, auditory, or cutaneous (touch) senses. One of the real virtues of sensory-tonic theory is that it is open to test. Unfortunately, experiments by different investigators do not consistently confirm the theoretical predictions. (See, for example, Weintraub, O'Connell, and McHale [1964].)

A more complex arrangement is that of Witkin's (1959) tilting-room–tilting-chair test. An observer is placed in a tilting chair inside a small room which can be tilted independently of the chair. He is asked either to adjust the room to upright or to adjust himself to an upright position. On the basis of their adjustments, people can be classified as "field dependent" and "field independent." The field-dependent observer's perception is dominated by the background and is influenced strongly by visual surroundings. Field-independent persons tend to differentiate objects from their surroundings and are therefore less influenced by the surroundings. It has been shown that other variables are related to field dependency versus field independency. Children tend to be field dependent, but they shift toward field independency as they mature. Women tend more toward field dependency than men. Field-independent people seem to have more complex personality organization, to prefer active striving when dealing with their environment, and to function with greater independence. As with kinesthetic aftereffects, a purely perceptual task—the determination of apparent verticality—appears to be predictive of a number of important variables outside the realm of perception.

THE EFFECTS OF ROTATION

At the U.S. Naval School of Aviation Medicine in Pensacola, Florida, an elaborate apparatus known as the Slow Rotation Room (Graybiel, Clark, and Zarriello, 1959) has been constructed. It is a completely enclosed circular room, 15 feet in diameter, 7 feet high, rotating around its vertical centerline. Most of the comforts of home are available, including sleeping, cooking, and toilet facilities, allowing subjects to live in the room continuously for several weeks. There are also books, taped music, and television. Although the effects of the earth's gravity cannot be eliminated, the rotation of the room provides an additional force in a direction outward from the center of rotation and perpendicular to the force of gravity. Visually, the environment is stable, the room is virtually vibration free, and all objects are rotating with the observer. However, any head turning or tilting movements about an axis other than that of the room's rotation disturb the fluid in the semicircular canals in a manner which would not occur in a stationary room. Visually, the environment is at rest; vestibularly, the environment is not at rest. Depending on the susceptibility of an observer, the revolutions per minute of the room, and the amount of head turning, an extreme and unpleasant form of motion sickness has been observed. It is called "canal sickness" because of the involvement of the semicircular canals. At high-rotation speeds, such as 10 rpm, almost all participants experience stomach disturbances, sweating, nausea, dizziness, apathy, difficulty in walking—many to the point of being incapacitated. Needless to say, the experimenter living aboard is also affected, and he sometimes proves unable to administer the many intellectual and motor tasks planned to assess the effects of rotation. Many subjects can adapt, fortunately, after days of sustained rotation. But on cessation of rotation, aftereffects similar to canal sickness itself are observed—drowsiness, irritability, difficulty in maintaining balance while walking, even nausea—and these may last for 48 hours or so. Observers learn to react properly with practice. If a subject stands near the center of rotation and tries to throw a ball into a basket located at the edge of the room, a considerable amount of lead in the direction of rotation is required. In essence, the basket is moving out from under the arc of the ball, and it is difficult to anticipate the amount of lead required at high rpm. The apparently curved flight of the ball must be experienced to be fully appreciated. When the room is stopped, observers still tend to lead their throws even though they "know" that motion has ceased. Many throws are required before the observers are able to hit the basket again with consistency.

If an observer sits in a chair at the outer edge of the room facing the direction of rotation and is asked to set a luminous line to horizontal, he can do this relatively well. However, when the lights are then extinguished so that only the luminous line is visible, it rapidly appears to change from its horizontal position. If the subject is asked to set the line back to the horizontal, he positions the line so that it is tilted inward, toward the center of rotation. The observer's apparent horizontal is not perpendicular to the force of gravity, but to the vector sum of gravity plus the centrifugal force, as in Figure 9.1. The effect has been named the oculogravic illusion.

During acceleration (while the rotation speed is increasing), an illusion is observed. An illuminated object, such as an outline of a cube or radial lines forming a star-shaped pattern, which is in completely dark

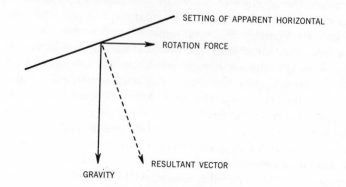

Figure 9.1

A vector diagram illustrating the oculogravic illusion.

surroundings and which is stationary with respect to the subject's head, will appear to move inward toward the center of rotation. Deceleration will cause motion in the opposite direction. In military aviation, during formation flying at night, this oculogyral illusion may have serious consequences. A wingman must hold his position with respect to the flight leader's lights; thus, a formation turn may induce the wingman to perceive that the leader is turning more sharply than he really is.

The acceleration or deceleration of rotation produces fluid movement in the semicircular canals and leads to the oculogyral illusion. At a constant rotation speed, some special and very curious forms of the oculogyral illusion have been observed. Tilting the head sets the fluid in motion, and in a well-lighted Slow Rotation Room, everything in the field of view may appear to swim before the eyes, providing an impression that the room is moving impossibly in many different directions. As subjects adapt to their rotating home, the illusion gradually subsides. In a completely dark environment rotating at constant rpm, when a subject tilts his head from an erect position toward a shoulder, a small illuminated target appears to move rapidly in a more or less vertical direction, then commences a slow motion back to its initial position. The direction of apparent motion is predictable. For example, if the subject is at the center of rotation, clockwise rotation with head tilt to the right produces an ascending target. The effect has been called the Vestibular Coriolis Reaction (Guedry and Montague, 1961). Though it may seem incredible, observers report that although the target appears to be moving rapidly, it doesn't appear to be going very far—as if speed and motion were divorced from one another. Judged velocity therefore does not coincide with judged displacement in this case, and subjects must be trained to report one or the other in order not to shift criteria in the middle of an experiment. One of the authors (D.J.W.) has experienced the phenomenon, and, paradoxical or not, the published reports coincide with his experience. Deaf observers with semicircular-canal abnormalities do not exhibit any forms of the oculogyral illusion.

We have very briefly illustrated the interaction possible between two sensory systems, trying at the same time to indicate the practical and immediate applications of perceptual investigation. Many illusions—such as the oculogyral illusion—are more than laboratory curiosities; perceptual experiments have wider application than the testing of theory.

The manner in which we perceive the world is plastic. It is subject to modification through learning, and can vary with circumstances. This chapter will briefly introduce some aspects of the plasticity, or malleability, of perception and will explore the relation of the topic of "perception" to other topics in psychology.

SOME GENERAL PROBLEMS OF THE RELATION OF PERCEPTION TO OTHER ASPECTS OF PSYCHOLOGY

In preceding chapters, "perception" has been treated as a special problem to be explored and investigated as an end in itself. It has been necessary, on occasion, to mention or discuss other psychological terms, such as learning; but the process of perception has been the focus of interest. For the most part, the problems and phenomena covered in the preceding chapters are often referred to as the area of "Classical Perception." It is "classical" in at least two senses: (1) the problems discussed were the first to be investigated experimentally, and (2) in general, the phenomena investigated represent "pure" perception, unaffected by factors other than the nature of the stimulus and the inherent characteristics of the perceiver.

In other volumes in this series and in this chapter, the terms "percept," "perception," and "to perceive" will be used with broader and more varied meanings, taking into account the influence on perception of such variables as learning, motivation, and social pressures. The growing interest of psychologists in such variables is sometimes referred to as the "new look" in perception. In order to discuss these developments, we must specify some of the current usages of the term "perception."

THREE USES OF THE TERM "PERCEPTION" IN BEHAVIOR THEORY

In *Psychology as a Natural and Social Science* (Walker, 1967), which deals with behavior theory, distinctions are made between subjectivity and objectivity, and between empirical and theoretical constructs. When "I" look out of my window and see a tree, the perception of the tree is a subjective experience. When I describe the experience, my description is objective; it can be matched with other descriptions and can be subjected to systematic analysis. From my own description or those of a number of observers, I might make logical inferences concerning "perception in general." In this example, the term "perception" has been used to mean three different things: (1) a subjective experience, which is not available to scientific investigation; (2) a set of descriptive statements, which are open to investigation; and (3) a construct about which theoretical statements may be made.

When the term perception is used to refer to a set of descriptive statements or when it is used to designate a theoretical construct, it is no longer confined to the obvious qualities of immediate perceptual experience. The next section will be an exploration of some of the ways in which the concept of perception has been broadened.

THE PENUMBRA OF THE CONCEPT OF PERCEPTION

In most situations discussed to this point, there is little ambiguity concerning the limits of what we have referred to as "perception" and "perceptual phenomena." However, these terms are frequently used in psychology in situations in which it is not so obvious that they are applicable. Let us explore this shadowy border of the meaning of the term *perception*.

NONSENSORY FIGURE-GROUND ORGANIZATION

As Hebb (1949) has pointed out, our perceptions are sometimes organized without benefit of sensory gradients or boundaries. While driving, most of us have a fairly clear perception of the appropriate distance that we should maintain between our own automobile and the one in front of us. Furthermore, the distance should and usually does vary with the speed. This "safety boundary" is real, is a part of our perception, and yet it is not fixed by a line or mark in the environment. There are many sports in which nonsensory boundaries contribute to perception. A golfer standing on a tee ready to drive has a clear perception of the length of a drive, and this figure-ground relationship is as real to him as if a line were in fact marked on the fairway at an appropriate distance. Thus, our perceptions can and do have boundaries which are not supported by sensory gradients.

PERCEPTION OF PERSONAL AND SOCIAL CHARACTERISTICS

The term *perception* is used in the areas of personality and social psychology. For example, there is "appropriate conversational distance"— although we are not always acutely aware of it, there is a distance we maintain in talking with another person. To test it, simply move closer to a person with whom you are in normal conversation, and one of two things is almost certain to happen: (1) the other person will back away in order to reestablish the appropriate distance, or (2) he or she will begin to show signs of discomfort. That we perceive such a boundary for social intercourse—and that it is unsupported by a sensory gradient or border—is certain. The actual distance varies with immediate and traditional circumstances. The appropriate distance to maintain in a conversation is different when meeting a person on a street than it might be in holding a conversation on a date on a dimly lighted porch or patio. Peoples from Mediterranean countries tend to stand closer together in conversation than do the peoples of Northern Europe.

Another use of the term perception occurs when personal and social characteristics themselves are spoken of as being a part of the percept. Thus it is possible to perceive someone as being angry. There may be nothing about the immediate appearance of the person that indicates anger, but knowledge of the situation or knowledge of prior events may still lead a person to perceive the person as being angry. Or a person might be perceived as being an authority figure or a leader without any formal symbol of authority or leadership present at the time. This use of the term perception follows naturally from the assumption that past experience, or knowledge, contributes to perception. If experience can lead one to perceive distance more accurately, then experience could be expected to contribute a quality such as anger to a given perception. Following this logic, one finds such personal and social characteristics described as learned attributes of perception.

PERCEPTION, AWARENESS, AND BEHAVIOR

The term perception is strongly identified with conscious awareness. If we are not aware of a stimulus, then we do not perceive that stimulus or the object from which it arises. Yet it can be shown that people respond differentially to some stimuli and yet are not able to report awareness of the stimuli. A clear example is a classic experiment reported by McCleary and Lazarus (1949). Out of a selected group of nonsense syllables, they associated some with shock. The nonsense syllables were then presented in a tachistoscope. The experimenters reported that subjects showed a higher galvanic skin reflex (GSR) to syllables associated with shock than to syllables not associated with shock, even when the subjects were unable to report correctly the syllables that had been exposed. If the McCleary and Lazarus results are taken at face value, then their subjects were identifying the nature of the stimulus with one kind of response, GSR, even when they were not able to identify it verbally and thus indicate conscious awareness of the nature of the stimulus. McCleary and Lazarus invented the label "subception" to apply to this phenomenon. There is not complete agreement among psychologists that discrimination without awareness has been demonstrated. Eriksen (1956, 1960) has been sharply critical of such findings on methodological grounds, and the relation of awareness to perception continues to be controversial.

In the previous paragraph, the term "conscious awareness" was used as if it were a fixed value. It takes little thought to call such a simple conception into question. For example, the McCleary and Lazarus subjects were unable to report the precise syllable that had been presented, but they undoubtedly perceived *something*. While they did not discriminate, as indicated by GSR, without conscious awareness or without perception, they apparently did sometimes discriminate without accurate perception of the syllable. Such an argument raises questions concerning the definitions of a threshold and of consciousness.

It is easy to think of thresholds as being absolute. That is, either one does detect a stimulus if it lies above threshold, or one does not, if it lies below threshold. Along with the idea of an absolute threshold goes the idea that the sensory mechanism has an absolute limit of sensitivity. Whether or not there is an absolute threshold, most psychologists are finding it more profitable to think of stimulus detection in graded rather than discrete terms. When thresholds are measured, no discrete threshold appears. There is always a range of stimulus values—from stimuli so weak that detection is no better than chance, through values detected with increasing probability, to values that are always detected. A "threshold" is an arbitrarily selected value of the stimulus, such as the intensity of stimulation that is detected exactly 50% of the time. This arbitrary value for the threshold will differ from subject to subject. It will differ with minor differences in the conditions under which the measurements are taken. It will differ with even minor differences in the nature of the response that the subject is asked to make, and it will differ widely between two widely different responses such as "accurate verbal report" and a "significant GSR."

As early as 1884, Peirce and Jastrow were able to show that subjects can discriminate between small weights even though they have no confidence that they really can tell the difference. In recent years, Blackwell (1958) has developed and employed a four-category, forced-choice technique of threshold measurement. The observer looks at a homogeneous white area (with small reference points to indicate the direction in which to look). Four time intervals are indicated by an auditory stimulus, and the observer is required to choose one of the intervals as the one in which a small spot of light appeared. It has been demonstrated that an observer can do much better than chance in choosing the right interval, even when he is quite certain that he saw nothing at all that represented the stimulus.

Thus one kind of verbal report, indicating one or another of the four intervals, can reveal detection of the stimulus; while another kind of verbal report, "awareness" of the stimulus, indicates that there is none. If the two verbal reports disagree, there certainly is nothing to prevent one from using GSR as the "perceptual response" to reveal detection of the presence of a "threatening" stimulus. (For a more detailed treatment of the problem and an introduction to modern signal-detection theory, see "Is there a sensory threshold? by Swets [1961]. For an introduction to the problems of measurement in psychology, see *Quantification in Psychology* by William L. Hays, a volume in this series. For a discussion of the many meanings of the word "conscious," see Miller [1942].)

Although there is no absolute threshold that can be demonstrated and no fixed level of awareness that is the boundary of consciousness, we still can use the words "subliminal" to mean below limen (threshold), and "unconscious" to mean below some criterion of conscious awareness. It is only necessary to keep in mind, when such words are used, that some specific criterion is implied.

In the sensory experiments discussed above, the observer is not "aware" of the stimulus because it is too weak, even though he is looking in its direction and exerting every effort to "see" and to become "aware" of it. There is another reason why a person might not be aware of a stimulus. A stimulus might be quite evident when one's attention is called to it—that is, it is considerably above any arbitrary threshold of detectability—but it may not enter awareness because of lack of attention. When asked "Did you notice the dress she wore?" you may reply in the negative if you are a man and if you failed to attend to the dress when you were looking at her. You did not become aware of the stimulus because you failed to attend to this stimulus. The question can then arise as to whether you can respond discriminately to stimuli of which you are not aware because of inattention.

Behavior without Awareness (from Inattention). A very early, but convincing, demonstration of the powers of attention in excluding clearly present stimuli is a study by Perky (1910). She had subjects working on a visual task and manipulated the intensity of another stimulus that was not involved in what the subject had to do. When later asked to describe the situation, subjects gave no hint of awareness of the irrelevant stimulus, even when it had been made quite intense.

That such stimuli can influence behavior has been demonstrated repeatedly. In two classic studies, unnoticed stimuli have been demonstrated to affect verbal behavior. Cohen *et al.* (1954) performed an experiment in which the experimenter casually said "Right" whenever the subject began a sentence with the word "I" or "We." The subjects increased the frequency with which they used such sentences. In a similar situation, Greenspoon (1955) said "mm-humm" after the subject used a plural noun. Repeated use of the approving vocal sound doubled the number of plural nouns used by his subjects. Subjects, in general, were unaware of the nature of the situation and perceived no relation between the approving comments and their own verbal behavior. Thus a clearly demonstrable relationship can be established between an aspect of the stimulus environment and a subject's behavior, without the subject being aware of the connection.

Behavior in Response to Stimuli of Which We Cannot Become Aware. We have discussed behavior in response to stimuli too weak to permit awareness, and to stimuli of which we are not aware because we did not attend to them. There are other stimuli to which we respond with precision even though they are ordinarily, and possibly always, unavailable to consciousness. For example, most of us are completely unaware of the afferent or sensory information provided by the vestibular sense, yet we ordinarily maintain our balance. Motor skills are probably partly developed from the kinesthetic sense, yet under most circumstances, we are not consciously aware of this sense. In *Sensory Processes,*[*] Wolsk discusses a variety of possible sensory inputs to the brain from the viscera, none of which are available to consciousness but all of which can and do serve to control behavior.

Perception in the Absence of External Stimulation. In the broadest sense of the word, what we "perceive" is jointly determined by the stimulus itself and by our relevant past experience. In some situations, however, past experience appears either wholly irrelevant or so universally common to all individuals that the stimulus seems to be all-important. There are other situations in which the stimulus plays a small role, and the percept seems wholly determined by past experience or some other element of the situation. Such percepts are usually attributed to a variable such as motivation or expectancy and are referred to as "imaginary" or "hallucinatory." (Some experimental examples will be treated later in this chapter.)

The hallucination is a dramatic instance of a perception without the support of a distal stimulus. To perceive something that is obviously (to others) not present in the stimulus is taken as a symptom of mental aberration. Under the influence of one of the "hallucinogenic" drugs, a person may perceive complex patterns without benefit of obvious external stimuli. There are a number of such drugs, the most common of which are mescaline and LSD. They have been used by certain Indian tribes of southwestern United States and of Mexico in ceremonial functions, by people seeking "kicks," and by some scientists as a tool in the investigation of mental illness. Ingestion of the drugs produces effects which are both remarkable and extremely dangerous. The locus of action of these drugs is believed to be directly upon portions of the nervous

---

[*] Alpern, Lawrence, and Wolsk, *Sensory Processes*, 1967, in this series.

system, and thus they cannot be regarded as stimuli in the ordinary sense of the word. The "perceptions" of a person so drugged certainly do not correspond to any distal stimulus patterns. An easily available and recent discussion of hallucinogenic drugs is one by Barron, Jarvik, and Bunnell (1964).

Subliminal Advertising. "Subliminal advertising" caused considerable public furor a few years ago when an advertising firm claimed that presentation of stimuli below the level of conscious awareness could induce people to buy a product. They reported that when the words "Eat Popcorn" or "Drink Coca-Cola" were flashed on a movie screen so briefly that no one in the audience noticed it, there was, nevertheless, a large increase in the sales of these products to the audience. The report was not presented in a form that could be verified, but public concern created great interest in the question of whether, and to what extent, behavior could be controlled by subliminal stimuli. The extent to which it can be "controlled" is a question that cannot be fully dealt with here. There are two excellent reviews of relevant problems. Adams (1957) has reviewed laboratory studies of behavior without awareness, and McConnell, Cutler, and McNeil (1958) have reviewed these and other studies relevant to the question of possible effectiveness of subliminal advertising.

SUMMARY OF THE PENUMBRA OF PERCEPTION

The concept of "perception," figuratively speaking, has a penumbra. We can clearly "perceive" a tree sharply outlined in good light. Yet it is also possible to talk about perception when there is no sensory gradient, when there is no external stimulus, when stimuli are too weak to permit a report of awareness, when stimuli are present but not attended to, and even to situations in which it is known that there are afferent inputs but we are structured in such a manner that we can never become directly aware of their presence or character. It might be better if words other than "perception" were used to refer to these aspects of our experience and behavior, but the term "perception" is frequently used to refer to the reaction of the person to a stimulus pattern even though he is not "aware" of its presence. And to illustrate still another sense, we also "perceive" a person as an authority figure.

SOME RELATIONS OF PERCEPTION TO OTHER PSYCHOLOGICAL CONCEPTS

It is clear that when we interpret perception as broadly as it has been interpreted in the preceding paragraphs, the study of perception is almost coextensive with the study of psychology. In this brief section, an attempt will be made to introduce the reader to some implications of such a broad interpretation.

First, we will make an arbitrary distinction between the effects on perception of events which occurred in the relatively remote past and of those which are present or occurred in the immediate past. Effects of events from the remote past will be termed learning, while effects of present events or events in the immediate past will be called motivation and social influences.

LEARNING AND PERCEPTION

The word "learning" has appeared repeatedly in reference to perception in this volume. There is still at least one more question upon which we might again focus our attention with profit. This is the question of whether we "learn" to perceive under any circumstances at all. Such a question is not easy to answer—any specific instance will be beset by problems and questions such as "Does our perception really undergo change as a function of learning, or do we merely learn to respond differently or more accurately to something we could perceive all along?" Perhaps the best and the most convincing answer would come from perceptual "learning" that the reader can probably demonstrate for himself.

We are probably the first people in history which has had no real need to live under low levels of illumination. With the proliferation of means of providing artificial illumination, most of us in the United States live almost constantly under high general illumination, or at worst, under conditions in which our path or immediate functional environment is highly illuminated. Thus most of us have the opportunity to learn to see in the dark or under low levels of illumination while being critically observant of the process. This is in contrast to our ancestors, who had to learn to do a great many things in the dark or under low levels of illumination, and for whom learning to see in the dark was something that happened gradually with normal development.

To carry out this perceptual learning experiment, all that is necessary is to arrange a place where you can be in the dark and awake for an hour or more at a time. A suitable environment might be the mountains after dark, without artificial illumination. Those of us who do not have the good fortune to have that opportunity or a similar natural one can create a suitable artificial situation.

During World War II, it became obvious to military authorities that many men had never learned to see under low levels of illumination, and that many of them, ranging from combat infantrymen to pilots of night intruder aircraft, would find it important to work effectively without artificial illumination. In response to this problem, night-vision trainers were constructed, and training programs were developed to aid men in learning to see at night. All of the necessary features of such a training program can be carried out in any ordinary room that can be brought to extremely low levels of illumination.

In a typical night-vision training program, men were either brought directly into a dark room or were given red goggles to wear for a period of 30 minutes or so before entering such a room. Alpern's chapter on vision in *Sensory Processes* ° discusses the enormous increase in sensitivity to light that occurs as a process of dark adaptation. Most of this increase in sensitivity takes place in the first 30 minutes in the dark. Wearing red goggles for 30 minutes is fairly effective because the rods are relatively insensitive to long wavelength red light compared to other wavelengths. The change in sensitivity that is most important for our purposes takes place with respect to the rods—receptors which are distributed around the periphery of the retina.

In the military training situation, men usually sat facing a screen at one end of a room. Any kind of scene or object might be projected on the screen—frequently a silhouette of trees, houses, and other objects, along with a few critical objects such as tanks, men, or even planes. The picture on the screen was always illuminated at such a low level that one had to be in the dark 30 or more minutes before one could even tell that there was an illuminated screen.

The normal experience under such circumstances is initially distressing—when you think you have spotted something out of the corner of your eye, you look toward it, and it disappears. Unless the problem is explained to you, it might take a long time to learn that you are essentially blind in the center of your field of vision under low levels of illumination, and that to see anything, you must look away from the point of interest by several degrees. This is necessary because the cones in the center of the retina are not sensitive at very low levels of illumination, and rods are relatively rare in this region.

Once the "trick" of viewing objects off-center is learned, then there is a progressive increase in the capacity to "see and to identify." Objects can be detected, described, and, if necessary, responded to. Often, men undergoing night-vision training report that moving objects are easier to perceive than stationary objects, or that it is easier to see a stationary object if you don't look at one small area too long. There is some possibility that the rods are especially sensitive to movement.

In any case, practice results in a very large increase in the capacity to "see in the dark," to identify and respond appropriately to objects. The question is: did any of the learning consist in pure learning to "perceive"?

It is clear that some improvement is the result of learning to look away from the object one wishes to "see." Some improvement may be a matter of learning appropriate eye movements. It is difficult to separate improvement that can be attributed to dark *adaptation* that may continue

---

° Alpern, Lawrence, and Wolsk, *op. cit.*

beyond the point at which you first begin to detect objects visually—from improvements which can be interpreted as *perceptual learning*. The reader is invited to arrange a situation and try it for himself. If he is careful and patient, and if he is good at analysis of his own subjective experience, the reader may be able to answer the question to his own satisfaction. One of the authors (E.L.W.), who served as a night vision training officer, is convinced that perceptual learning does occur under these circumstances.

A more objective demonstration of perceptual learning can be made in the area of the perception of words. If one successively flashes a variety of words on a screen—in a manner that permits measurement of the threshold for correct perception, the threshold will be found to vary as a function of several quantitative aspects of the words used. One of the most important determiners of the threshold is the frequency of usage of the word. Thorndike and Lorge (1944) have developed a list of 30,000 English words rated in terms of the frequency with which they appear in newspapers and books. With other factors held constant, the recognition thresholds for words can be shown to be relatively low for words that occur frequently and to be relatively high for words that occur infrequently. For a discussion of frequency of usage as it affects the visibility and auditory intelligibility of words refer to Rosenzweig and Postman (1958).

Admission of the likelihood that perceptual learning does occur raises an interesting paradox. The idea that our perception should be a faithful representation of the stimulus seems to conflict with the idea that perception is determined, in part, by past experience. To the extent to which experience is a factor in perception, one might expect the percept to fail to correspond to the distal stimulus. Gibson and Gibson (1955) present a discussion of this problem, in which they point out that perceptual learning can lead to increased differentiation of the stimulus, progressive elaboration of the qualities, features, and dimensions of variation in the stimulus, and thus to progressively *greater* correspondence with the stimulus. For instance, when we learn to see under very low levels of illumination, learning consists of greater and greater capacity to discriminate the true character of the stimulus. It seems likely that this position, stated by the Gibsons, is correct. Regardless of the stage of perceptual learning, the character of the distal stimulus is primary in determining the nature of the perception.

MEMORY

Closely related to the problem of perceptual learning is the problem of what happens to a percept when the distal stimulus is removed, in other words, what happens to perception in memory. If there are *systematic distortions* in visual memory for form, as has been argued by

Gestalt psychologists, the problem is an important one. For example, Koffka (1935) states a widely held position that memorial changes can be described as (1) *normalization* or *closure,* which consists of changes that approach a more simple or a more familiar figure (2) *pointing* or *sharpening,* which consists of exaggerations of certain characteristics of the figure, and (3) *autonomous changes* within the memory trace, as a result of intrinsic stress in the visual pattern. A straightforward experimental test of these propositions is somewhat more difficult than it might appear. If a subject is asked to draw a visual form from memory, his production can be distorted because of (1) changes in the memory trace; (2) simple lack of drawing skill, commonly referred to in this context as productive error; or (3) reproductive error—if the person is asked to draw the same form from memory several times. There is a study by Walker and Veroff (1956) in which productive error, reproductive error, and dynamic changes in the memory trace are independently determined. The researchers conclude that there are dynamic changes in the memory trace for form, but that it is doubtful whether all of the changes can be categorized simply, or whether the character of the changes that will occur can be predicted on the basis of our present knowledge.

MOTIVATION AND PERCEPTION

It is reasonable to ask how perception is influenced by motivation. A brief introduction to experimental studies of this relationship follows.

Perception as Determined in Part or Solely by Appetitive Motivation. If we think of some perceptions as being jointly determined by a distal stimulus and the immediate past history of the perceiver, we may ask whether it is possible to achieve something like perception in the absence of any identifiable distal stimulus. Thus one might make subjects hungry by depriving them of food; project pictures on a screen; and ask the subjects what they see. If the picture is wholly clear, it may be seen to be a curved stick. If the illumination is reduced, or if the exposure of the picture is very brief, the image may be seen as a banana or a hotdog. If the subject is led to believe that a picture had appeared when, in fact, there was no stimulus at all, he may report that he "saw" any number of objects, most of which will be some variety of food. No one has carried out this experiment exactly as described, but there are a number of similar experiments. Sanford (1937) performed one of the earliest experiments of this type and showed that subjects who had been deprived of food were more prone to produce "food-relevant" responses to a series of ambiguous stimuli. McClelland and Atkinson (1948) found an increase in the frequency of certain hunger-related responses in food-deprived subjects who were asked to write stories about ambiguous pictures. Thus, it seems clear that a motive state such as hunger can influence the nature of perception of ambiguous stimuli.

Perception as Influenced by Fear. That fear can influence perception is almost beyond dispute. A child left alone will hear footsteps coming up the stairs when the objective stimulus may be something so remotely different as a steady drip of water. Yet experimental demonstrations of the role of fear in perception are rather difficult to achieve, largely because of the difficulty of, and ethical problems related to, the experimental production of fear. Fear usually comes when something unexpected happens, and is thus difficult to anticipate.

One of the authors (E.L.W.) had an unusual opportunity a few years ago to study fear in a planned situation. As a part of a military training exercise, troops were to be placed in trenches very close to the point at which an atomic explosion was to be produced. The position was closer than men had voluntarily occupied before, or since, and the setting was one in which distances appear extremely short. The net effect was that the participants, including the writer, felt that they were sitting virtually beneath an atomic bomb when it was to be detonated. In this setting, it was possible to carry out an experiment in which men were asked to write stories about characters in ambiguous pictures containing human figures. Furthermore, a similar task could be asked of the same or similar individuals removed in time both before and after the experience, and removed in distance from the site of the explosion. Fear-related stories were most frequently written in groups near the explosion in space and time. One can infer that fear induced by the situation affected what the men perceived when they looked at the ambiguous pictures (see Walker and Atkinson, 1958).

Perceptual Distortion of a Present Stimulus. The examples given so far, of the influence of motivation on perception, have involved motivational contributions to vague, ambiguous, or wholly absent stimuli. It is occasionally claimed that the perception of a clear and unambiguous stimulus can be distorted by motivational factors. Bruner and Goodman (1947) have reported that young children saw coins as being about 25% larger than cardboard discs which were actually the same size, and that poor children overestimate the size of coins more than rich children. The inference is that the value of the coin and the need for money each operated to "inflate" the perceived size of the coins. The finding has been challenged on several grounds. It has been pointed out that filled space (the coins) looks larger than unfilled space (the discs), a factor which is not regarded as motivational in character (see Figure 4.6 in Chapter 4). Carter and Schooler (1949) tried replication of the Bruner and Goodman study and found the judgment of coins to be accurate if the coins were present, but to be inflated if judgment was from memory. While the challenges and criticisms point up the need for rigid experimental control, and while they question the degree to which the direct perception of an unambiguous stimulus can be distorted, there seems little doubt that motivation can influence such perceptions if there is a degree of ambiguity or remoteness from the stimulus.

MOTIVATION AND PERCEPTUAL SELECTION

It seems clear to most of us that if one is hungry, one is more likely to notice food than if one is not hungry. We would describe this behavior as "perceptual selection." Anyone who has ever found money may have occasion to be puzzled as to why they managed to identify the coin when they did not identify the bottle caps, stones, papers, and other debris which might have been in the area. The experience is commonly one of the coin suddenly "standing out" from its background.

An analogous experimental test of this "standing out" character of need-related objects has been reported by Atkinson and Walker (1956). They measured *need for affiliation* in a large group of students. In the study, the students were divided into two groups—high and low need for affiliation. All subjects were then shown a series of pictures flashed on a screen at a speed that made it almost impossible to distinguish the true character of the pictures. Each picture actually consisted of four forms, arranged above, below, to the right, or the left of a central fixation point. One of the four forms was always a face, and the other three were similar forms but of inanimate objects. Each time a picture was flashed on the screen, the subjects were asked to indicate the position of the object that "stood out the most." Subjects who made high scores on the test for need for affiliation saw faces "standing out" much more frequently than those who had low scores on the test. This study appears to be a clear demonstration that variation in a social motive directly affects perceptual selection.

PERCEPTION AND SOCIAL BEHAVIOR

The need for affiliation is a social motive, but the behavior of perceptual selection of faces is not social behavior. When social behavior is involved, one immediately must tackle the problem of whether the perception has been affected, the social behavior has been affected, or both. What can be done is to contrive a situation in which it can be demonstrated that different people, with different motives, perceive a single situation differently depending upon their motivation.

A revelant study, of behavior based on a conflict in motives, is reported by Walker and Heyns (1962). Measures of need for achievement and need for affiliation were taken in a large group of female university students. The achievement motive is considered to represent the strength of the tendency toward striving to meet internalized standards of excellence; the affiliation motive is considered to be the need to establish and maintain strong contacts with friends. The two motives appear to be relatively independent, both in terms of common sense and in terms of the scores that individuals receive on the two tests. From these scores, it was possible to divide the subjects into four groups; those who (1) achieved high scores in both needs; (2) had high scores in need for achievement and low scores in need for affiliation; (3) had low scores in need for achievement and high scores in need for affiliation; (4) achieved low scores on both tests. The fourth group was not used further, since no prediction could be made about them.

The next step was to construct a situation that the subjects would perceive as achievement-relevant and affiliation-relevant, and one in which it would be clear whether performance was in response to the need for achievement or in response to the need for affiliation. The subjects were asked to bring a friend to participate in an experiment, since the experiment involved teamwork between pairs. When the subjects arrived, each pair was divided, with one member being sent to one room, and the other member sent to another. About ten pairs were scheduled at a time, so that there were about ten subjects in each of the rooms. Even though subjects were told the two groups were being treated differently, they were treated exactly the same.

They were first given a task that was assumed to arouse need for affiliation. Each subject was asked to indicate, on a list of personal traits, the extent to which each trait (such as sympathetic, dominant, cheerful, friendly, compliant, hostile, warm, suspicious, approval-seeking, and trusting) applied to herself and to her friend, and also how she thought her friend would be rating her.

Each subject was then given a task designed to arouse a high need for achievement. The task was to encode as many words as possible, following a strict coding formula, in a three minute period, and was presented as a contest to see who within the group could encode the largest number of words within a time limit. The group was told there would be six such contests.

It was further explained that after the first work period, the list of words that had been encoded would be taken across the hall where the partner was waiting. During the second work period the partner would have the task of unscrambling this list of words or decoding as many of them as possible. It was alleged that the friend was in a competition in which her score would be the percentage of the list she received that she succeeded in unscrambling. Thus the partner's task was made the more difficult the larger the number of words encoded by the subject. The friend's competitive situation was mentioned in the original instructions but was not stressed at the time.

At the end of the second contest, what was represented as the partner's first effort was returned to the subject. She was asked to check the list to be sure that the partner had recovered the correct word and then to calculate the percentage that was correctly decoded. The list which was returned to the subject at this point was, of course, not genuine. A number of such lists had been prepared in advance with varying numbers of supposedly decoded words on them. The experimenters merely collected the products of the first work period of the subjects, chose a list of decoded words from the prepared supply that was about half as long as the list encoded by each subject. The fake list was returned to the subject for checking and scoring and was presented as being the product of the partner's efforts. These lists were hand printed to eliminate the problem of recognition of handwriting.

At the end of the fourth work period, the list returned to the subject was like the previous ones, but it bore a request, presumably from the friend, *to please slow down*. At the end of the fifth trial, the subjects were told that the sixth trial would be the last, and that their friends would not be required to decode the words encoded on this last trial.

The subjects were thus in a conflict situation, the structure of which is pictured in Figure 10.1. The fact that they were asked to come ac-

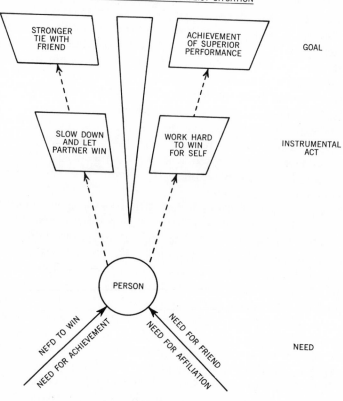

Figure 10.1

Structure of the conflict situation. (Adapted by permission from Walker and Heyns, An Anatomy for Conformity *[1962].)*

companied by a friend, the rating scheme they were asked to apply to themselves and the friend, and the supposed appeal from the friend to slow down, all were intended to engage the need for affiliation. That the experiment was carried out in a classroom and was presented as a contest was certain to engage the need for achievement. Thus, while the situation was the same for everyone, it could be perceived differently depending upon the motivational predisposition of the individual. Furthermore, there were two different and incompatible ways to behave depending upon how the situation was perceived. One could either work as fast and as hard as possible in an effort to achieve personal goals or slow down in an effort to permit the partner to achieve success. If one slowed down, one's partner would have a shorter list to work on, and thus had a chance of getting a larger percentage of the words unscrambled. The goals are also clear. One could achieve personal success and its satisfactions, or one could contribute to stronger ties with the friend, but one could not do both.

The clearest indication of how the situation is perceived, choice of instrumental act, and thus choice of goal, is the extent to which the group and the individual yielded to the pressure of the appeal to slow down after the fourth trial, and then speeded up again when this pressure was removed after the fifth. The group as a whole did show the effect of social pressure and slow down on the fifth trial, and performance did rise again on the sixth.

The more important issue, however, is whether individuals behaved differently in this situation depending upon how they perceived the situation—as a contest in which achievement was important, or as a situation in which it was important to aid and abet a friend. The three diagrams in Figure 10.2 indicate the results. In the bottom diagram, there is a fairly even split in performance among these individuals who were high in both needs. Slightly over half continued to work hard and the remainder slowed down in response to the appeal from the friend. As shown in the upper left diagram, about three-fourths of those who were high in need for achievement and low in need for affiliation continue to work hard to achieve personal success in spite of the appeal, while in the upper right diagram it is shown that about three-fourths of those who were high in need for affiliation and low in need for achievement slowed down in response to the appeal.

It is clear that individuals responded differently depending upon motivational predispositions. We infer that *perceptual selection* affected the subjects' responses—that they perceived the situation differently depending on the same motivational predispositions. Since it was affiliative versus achievement behavior that was measured directly, the effect of motivation on perception must remain an inference in this case. However, the reasonableness of the inference, of a change in *perception* as a result of social pressure, can be examined in two classic experiments.

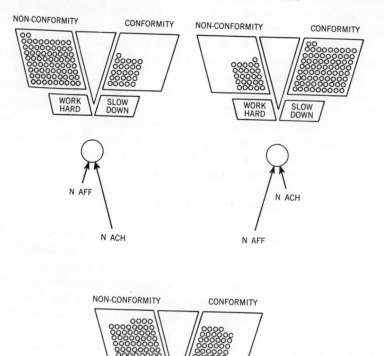

Figure 10.2

Performance in the conflict situation depending upon need strength. The diagram at the bottom represents the performance of subjects high in both need for achievement and need for affiliation. The upper right diagram represents the performance of those high in need for affiliation and low in need for achievement. The upper left diagram represents the performance of those high in need for achievement and low in need for affiliation. (Adapted by permission from Walker and Heyns [1962].)

In a dark room, a tendency exists for a stationary point of emitted light to be perceived as moving eccentrically. Sherif (1937) demonstrated that this perceptual experience, called the *autokinetic* effect, could be modified through the application of group pressure. If you have ever experienced the autokinetic effect, you will have little doubt that Sherif's subjects actually underwent a modification of their *perceptual* experience as a result of social pressure.

In a brilliantly conceived and executed set of experiments, Asch (1955) has shown that social pressure influences an individual's judgment of the length of a line. In a typical experiment, he would present to a group of seven or eight people two cards. One card had a single line (the standard) and the other card might have three lines, one of which was equal in length to the standard line and two of which were quite obviously different. The subjects would be asked to choose one of the three lines on the second card, and to report their judgments in the order in which they were seated. Through five or six trials, all would choose the correct line. Then by prearrangement, all but the last person would choose a line that was obviously different from the standard. Many subjects, in such a situation, would go along with the unanimous majority, and choose a line which was obviously discrepant. However, it is doubtful if many such subjects actually *perceived* the line as being different, even though their choice behavior was influenced by the majority.

Thus, it appears that in the Sherif experiments, the perception is actually modified, and the behavior of reporting the experience actually corresponds with the perception. In the Asch experiments, it is likely that the reporting behavior is affected without real modification in perception. The difference probably lies in the degree of ambiguity of the stimulus. If the stimulus is sufficiently clear and unambiguous, it is doubtful that perception of it can be grossly modified through motivation or social pressure. However, when the stimulus situation permits, either factor can apparently be a powerful determiner of perception.

PERCEPTUAL BEHAVIOR THEORY

While most general theories of behavior give a secondary role to perception, there are theories of a more or less general character that place the concept of perception in a prominent position. Such theories tend to deal with stimuli as they affect perception, and treat behavior as being determined, essentially, by the nature of perception.

An example of such a theory, at least in its initial stages of development, is that of Dember and Earl (Dember, 1960), who regard the complexity of a stimulus as one of its most important characteristics. With respect to any set of stimuli with which the individual might be faced, he will have a *preferred* or *ideal* complexity level. If he is given a free choice, he will choose to attend to or to interact with the preferred stimulus. In their theory, any stimulus that is less complex than the ideal will never be chosen. A stimulus slightly more complex than the ideal will eventually be chosen and will thus become the ideal. The slightly more complex stimulus is referred to as the *pacer* stimulus. Thus, as the individual continually or repeatedly interacts with a set of stimuli, he will come to choose stimuli which are progressively more complex by objective standards.

While the theory appears to be simple, it is broader in scope and applicability than it would initially appear: (1) Many stimuli can be categorized in terms of degree of choice. (2) A theory of motivation is implied by the concept of pacer stimulus. (3) A theory of learning is implied by the progressive change in preference. (4) There are many well known sequences in human behavior which seem to fit the pattern of development outlined by the theory. For example, musicians frequently progress from preferring simple melodies to preferring more complex music. A similar progression can be seen in preferences for literature or for works of art. How far the Dember and Earl theory can be extended to other psychological phenomena and problems remains to be seen.

Another general theory in which perceptual phenomena are given an extensive treatment is that of Berlyne (1960). He gives the concept of "arousal" a central role. The degree of arousal is largely a function of (1) perceptual variables such as novelty, surprisingness, and complexity, and (2) properties of an individual. The individual is conceived as seeking an *optimal arousal level,* and under certain conditions a little more than optimum. *Curiosity* is defined in terms of the motivation involved in seeking optimum arousal through interaction with stimulus characteristics such as complexity. In elaborated form, Berlyne's theory is able to deal with a great many of the problems of behavior that are of interest in psychology.

One of the present authors has recently published a third theory (Walker, 1964) which is in some sense an elaboration of those of Dember and Earl, and of Berlyne. In this theory, a distinction is made between stimulus complexity and psychological complexity. The theory states that although the complexity of a stimulus does not change, the psychological reaction to it will generally become less complex with continued experience. Further, an individual is motivated to seek optimum psychological complexity. This theory, too, contains a theory of learning and a theory of motivation.

If the concept of perception is interpreted to have wide application, and if the plasticity of perception is accepted, perceptual behavior theories may be developed into a general theory which can deal with a large majority of the problems that interest psychologists.

REFERENCES

Adams, J. K. Laboratory studies of behavior without awareness. *Psychol. Bull.*, 1957, *54*, 383–405.

Allport, G. A., and Pettigrew, T. F. Cultural influence on the perception of movement: The trapezoidal illusion among Zulus. *J. abn. soc. Psychol.*, 1957, *55*, 104–113.

Alpern, M., Lawrence, M., and Wolsk, D. *Sensory processes.* Belmont: Brooks/Cole, 1967.

Asch, S. E. Opinions and social pressure. *Sci. Amer.*, 1955, *193*, 31–35.

Atkinson, J. W., and Walker, E. L. The affiliation motive and perceptual sensitivity to faces. *J. abn. soc. Psychol.*, 1956, *53*, 38–41.

Bakan, P., Myers, L. B., and Schoonard, J. Kinesthetic after-effects and length of inspection-period. *Amer. J. Psychol.*, 1962, *75*, 457–461.

Barron, F., Jarvik, M. E., and Bunnell, S., Jr. The hallucinogenic drugs. *Sci. Amer.*, 1964, *210*, 29–38.

Berkeley, G. *An essay towards a new theory of vision.* 1709.

Berlyne, D. E. *Conflict, arousal, and curiosity.* New York: McGraw-Hill, 1960.

Blackwell, H. R. Personal communication. 1958.

Bruner, J. S. On perceptual readiness. *Psychol. Rev.*, 1957, *64*, 123–152.

——————, and Goodman, C. C. Value and need as organizing factors in perception. *J. abn. soc. Psychol.*, 1947, *42*, 33–44.

Brunswik, E. Representative design and probability theory in a functional psychology. *Psychol. Rev.*, 1955, *62*, 193–217.

Butter, C. M. *Neuropsychology: The study of brain and behavior.* Belmont: Brooks/Cole, 1967.

Carter, L. F., and Schooler, K. Value, need, and other factors in perception. *Psychol. Rev.*, 1949, *56*, 200–207.

Charles, L. P., and Duncan, C. P. The distance gradient in kinesthetic figural after-effect. *J. exp. Psychol.*, 1959, *57*, 164–170.

Cohen, B. D., Kalish, H. I., Thurston, J. R., and Cohen, E. Experimental manipulation of verbal behavior. *J. exp. Psychol.*, 1954, *47*, 106–110.

Cohen, J., and Gordon, D. A. The Prevost-Fechner-Benham subjective colors. *Psychol. Bull.*, 1949, *46*, 97–136.

Condillac, Étienne Bonnot de. *Traité des sensations.* 1754.

Dember, W.N. *Perception.* New York: Holt, 1960.

————————. *The psychology of perception.* New York: Holt, 1960.

DeValois, R. L. Color vision mechanisms in the monkey. *J. genet. Physiol.* (2nd supplement, mechanisms of vision), 1960, *43,* 115–128.

Diderot, Denis. *Lettre sur les aveugles.* 1749.

Duncker, K. The influence of past experience upon perceptual properties. *Amer. J. Psychol.,* 1939, *52,* 255–265.

Edwards, W., and Boring, E. G. What is Emmert's law? *Amer. J. Psychol.,* 1951, *64,* 416–422.

Eriksen, C. W. Subception: Fact or artifact? *Psychol. Rev.,* 1956, *63,* 74–80.

————————. Discrimination and learning without awareness: A methodological survey and evaluation. *Psychol. Rev.,* 1960, *67,* 279–300.

Evans, R. M. *An introduction to color.* New York: Wiley, 1948.

Gibson, J. J. Adaptation, after-effect, and contrast in the perception of curved lines. *J. exp. Psychol.,* 1933, *16,* 1–31.

————————. *The perception of the visual world.* Boston: Houghton Mifflin, 1950a.

————————. The perception of visual surfaces. *Amer. J. Psychol.,* 1950b, *63,* 367–384.

————————. Perception as a function of stimulation. In S. Koch (ed.), *Psychology: A Study of a science.* New York: McGraw-Hill, 1959, *1,* 456–501.

————————, and Gibson, Eleanor J. Perceptual learning: Differentiation or enrichment. *Psychol. Rev.,* 1955, *62,* 32–41.

Graybiel, A., Clark, B., and Zarriello, J. J. *Observations on human subjects living in a "slow rotation room" for periods of two days: Canal sickness.* U.S. Naval School of Aviation Medicine, Pensacola, Fla.: Research Project MROO5. 13–601 Subtask 1 Report #49, 1959.

Greenspoon, J. The reinforcing effect of two spoken sounds on the frequency of two responses. *Amer. J. Psychol.,* 1955, *68,* 409–416.

Guedry, F. E., Jr., and Montague, E. K. Quantitative evaluation of the vestibular coriolis reaction. *Aerospace Med.,* 1961, *32,* 487–500.

Hammer, E. R. Temporal factors in figural after-effects. *Amer. J. Psychol.,* 1949, *62,* 337–354.

Hays, W. L. *Quantification in psychology.* Belmont: Brooks/Cole, 1967.

Hebb, D. O. *The organization of behavior.* New York: Wiley, 1949.

Helson, H. Fundamental problems in color vision: I. The principle governing changes in hue, saturation, and lightness of non-selective samples in chromatic illumination. *J. exp. Psychol.,* 1938, *23,* 439–476.

————————. Adaptation level theory. In S. Koch (ed.), *Psychology: A study of a science.* New York: McGraw-Hill, 1959, *1,* 565–621.

————————. *Adaptation level theory.* New York: Harper, 1964.

Hochberg, J. E., Triebel, W., and Seaman, G.   Color adaptation under conditions of homogeneous visual stimulation (Ganzfeld). *J. exp. Psychol.*, 1951, *41*, 153–159.

Holway, A. H., and Boring, E. G.   Determinants of apparent visual size with distance variant. *Amer. J. Psychol.*, 1941, *54*, 21–37.

Hubel, D. H., and Wiesel, T. N.   Receptive fields of cells in the striate cortex of very young, visually inexperienced kittens. *J. Neurophysiol.*, 1963, *26*, 994–1002.

Judd, C. H.   Practice and its effects on the perception of illusions. *Psychol. Rev.*, 1902, *9*, 27–39.

Judd, D. B.   Appraisal of Land's work on two primary-color projections. *J. opt. Soc. Amer.*, 1960, *50*, 254–268.

Kaufman, L., and Rock, I.   The moon illusion. *Sci. Amer.*, 1962 (July), *207*, 120–130.

Koffka, K.   *Principles of Gestalt psychology.* New York: Harcourt, Brace, 1935, pp. 493–506.

Köhler, W.   *Gestalt psychology.* New York: Liveright, 1929.

——————, and Wallach, H.   Figural after-effects: An investigation of visual process. *Proc. Amer. phil. Soc.*, 1944, *88*, 269–357.

Kohler, I.   Experiments with goggles. *Sci. Amer.*, 1962 (May), *206*, 62–72.

Künnapas, T. M.   An analysis of the "vertical-horizontal illusion." *J. exp. Psychol.*, 1955, *49*, 134–140.

Land, E. H.   Experiments in color vision. *Sci. Amer.*, 1959 (May), *200*, 84–99.

Lashley, K. S., Chow, K. L., and Semmes, J.   An examination of the electrical field theory of cerebral integration. *Psychol. Rev.*, 1951, *58*, 123–136.

Leibnitz, Gottfried Wilhelm.   *La monadologie.* (Written in 1714.)

Manis, M.   *Cognitive processes.* Belmont: Brooks/Cole, 1966.

McCleary, R. A., and Lazarus, R. S.   Autonomic discrimination without awareness: An interim report. *J. Pers.*, 1949, *18*, 171–179.

McClelland, D. C., and Atkinson, J. W.   The projective expression of needs: I. The effect of different intensities of the hunger drive on perception. *J. Psychol.*, 1948, *25*, 205–222.

McConnell, J. V., Cutler, R. L., and McNeil, E. B.   Subliminal stimulation: An overview. *Amer. Psychol.*, 1958, *13*, 229–242.

Miller, J. G.   *Unconsciousness.* New York: Wiley, 1942.

Osgood, C. E.   *Method and theory in experimental psychology.* New York: Oxford, 1953.

Panum, P. L.   *Physiologische Untersuchungen über das Sehen mit zwei Augen.* 1858.

Peirce, C. S., and Jastrow, J.   On small differences of sensation. *Mem. nat. Acad. Sci.*, 1884, *3*, 75–83.

Perky, C. W. An experimental study of imagination. *Amer. J. Psychol.*, 1910, *21*, 422–452.

Petrie, A. Some psychological aspects of pain and the relief of suffering. *Ann. N.Y. Acad. Sci.*, 1960, *86*, 13–27.

Postman, L., and Tolman, E. C. Brunswik's probabilistic functionalism. In S. Koch (ed.), *Psychology: A study of a science*, New York: McGraw-Hill, 1959, *1*, 502–564.

Prentice, W. C. H. The systematic psychology of Wolfgang Köhler. In S. Koch (ed.), *Psychology: A study of a science*. New York: McGraw-Hill, 1959, *1*, 427–455.

Riesen, A. H. Plasticity of behavior: Psychological series. In H. F. Harlow and C. N. Woolsey (eds.), *Biological and biochemical bases of behavior*. Madison: University of Wisconsin Press, 1950, pp. 425–450.

Rosenzweig, M. R., and Postman, L. Frequency of usage and the perception of words. *Science*, 1958, *127*, 263–266.

Rubin, E. Figure and ground. In D. C. Beardslee and M. Wertheimer (eds.), *Readings in perception*. Princeton: Van Nostrand, 1958, pp. 194–203.

Sagara, M., and Oyama, T. Experimental studies on figural after-effects in Japan. *Psychol. Bull.*, 1957, *54*, 327–338.

Sanford, R. N. The effects of abstinence from food upon imaginal processes: A further experiment. *J. Psychol.*, 1937, *3*, 145–159.

Sherif, M. An experimental approach to the study of attitudes. *Sociometry*, 1937, *I*, 90–98.

Sickles, W. R. Experimental evidence for the electrical character of visual fields derived from a quantitative analysis of the Ponzo illusion. *J. exp. Psychol.*, 1942, *30*, 84–91.

Stratton, G. M. Vision without inversion of the retinal image. *Psychol. Rev.*, 1897, *4*, 341–360.

Swets, J. A. Is there a sensory threshold? *Science*, 1961, *134*, 168–177.

Thorndike, E. L., and Lorge, I. *The teacher's word book of 30,000 words*. New York: Teacher's College, Columbia University, 1944.

Vinci, da, Leonardo. *Trattato della pittura*. c. 1500 (edition used, 1735; German translation, 1882, vol. 2).

Von Senden, M. *Raum-und Gestaltauffassung bei operierten Blindgebornen vor und nach der Operation*. Leipzig: Barth, 1932. (An English translation is available: *Space and sight*. Glencoe, Ill.: Free Press, 1960.)

Walker, E. L. Psychological complexity as a basis for a theory of motivation and choice. In D. Levins (ed.), *Nebraska Symposium on Motivation*. Lincoln, Nebraska: University of Nebraska Press, 1964.

————. *Conditioning and instrumental learning*. Belmont: Brooks/Cole, 1967.

————. *Psychology as a natural and social science*. Belmont: Brooks/Cole, 1967.

——————, and Atkinson, J. W. The expression of fear-related motivation in thematic apperception as a function of proximity to an atomic explosion. In J. W. Atkinson (ed.), *Motives in fantasy, action and society*. Princeton, N.J.: Van Nostrand, 1958.

——————, and Heyns, R. W. *An anatomy for conformity*. Englewood Cliffs, N.J.: Prentice-Hall, 1962.

——————, and Veroff, J. Changes in the memory-trace for perceived forms with successive reproductions. *Amer. J. Psychol.*, 1956, *69*, 395–402.

Walls, G. L. Land! Land! *Psychol. Bull.*, 1960, *57*, 29–48.

Weintraub, D. J., O'Connell, D. C., and McHale, T. J. Apparent verticality: Fundamental variables of sensory-tonic theory reinvestigated. *J. exp. Psychol.*, 1964, *68*, 550–554.

Werner, H., and Wapner, S. Toward a general theory of perception. *Psychol. Rev.*, 1952, *59*, 324–338.

Wertheimer, M. Principles of perceptual organization. In D. C. Beardslee and M. Wertheimer (eds.), *Readings in perception*. Princeton: Van Nostrand, 1958, pp. 115–135.

Wheatstone, C. R. *Soc. London Philos. Trans.* 1838, pp. 371–394.

Wiesel, T. N., and Hubel, D. H. Single-cell responses in striate cortex of kittens deprived of vision in one eye. *J. Neurophysiol.*, 1963, *26*, 1003–1017.

Witkin, H. A. The perception of the upright. *Sci. Amer.*, 1959 (Feb.) *200*, 50–56.

Woodworth, R. S. *Experimental psychology*. New York: Holt, 1938.

——————, and Schlosberg, H. *Experimental psychology* (revised edition). New York: Holt, 1954.

NAME INDEX

SUBJECT INDEX